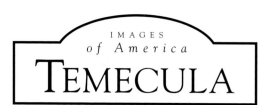

IMAGES
of America

TEMECULA

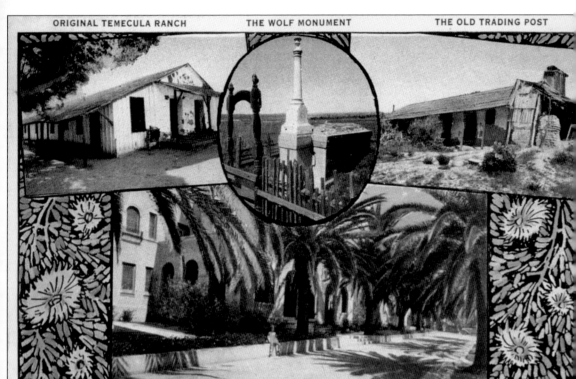

A PLEASANT RETREAT AT GUENTHER'S MURRIETA MINERAL HOT SPRINGS, MURRIETA, CALIF.

POSTCARD IMAGES OF EARLY TEMECULA. These four landmarks signify important aspects of Temecula history. The Wolf Store adobe, labeled "Original Temecula Ranch," stands on Highway 79 South next to Kohl's Department Store. The Temecula Valley Historical Society has recently restored the Wolf Monument in Wolf Valley. Remaining are a few crumbling adobe walls of the Old Trading Post, also known as the Second Magee Store. Fritz Guenther opened Guenther's Murrieta Hot Springs Resort, a once famous health resort that is now a Bible college. (Courtesy of VaRRA.)

ON THE COVER: The verdant land and ample water supply attracted people to the region. These resources first sustained the Temecula Indians, then caught the eyes of padres from Mission San Luis Rey, who set up an outpost for raising grain for mission herds. As sheep and cattle ranchers moved in, the lush grain harvests produced food for the animals. The haying crew in this 1890s photograph is posing on the Pauba Ranch with a baling machine. (Courtesy of Peggy Goffman.)

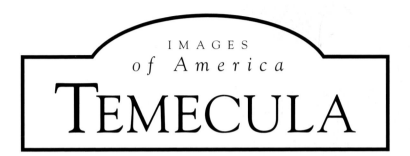

IMAGES
of America

TEMECULA

Loretta Barnett, Rebecca Farnbach,
and the Vail Ranch Restoration Association

ARCADIA
PUBLISHING

ISBN 0-7385-3095-6

Published by Arcadia Publishing
Charleston SC, Chicago IL, Portsmouth NH, San Francisco CA

Printed in the United States of America

Library of Congress Catalog Card Number: 2005934842

For all general information contact Arcadia Publishing at:
Telephone 843-853-2070
Fax 843-853-0044
E-mail sales@arcadiapublishing.com
For customer service and orders:
Toll-Free 1-888-313-2665

Visit us on the Internet at www.arcadiapublishing.com

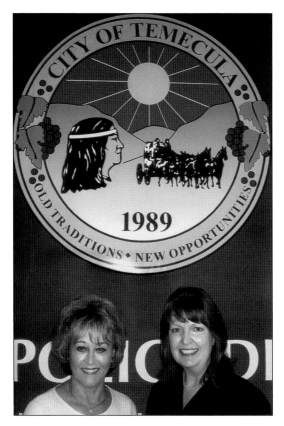

CITY SEAL. Authors Loretta Barnett and Rebecca Farnbach are pictured with the seal of the City of Temecula, incorporated in 1989. The seal represents the people who first lived here, the wineries of the valley, and the Butterfield Stage Route that once passed through. (Courtesy of VaRRA.)

CONTENTS

ACKNOWLEDGMENTS

The Vail Ranch Restoration Association (VaRRA) thanks the Roripaugh Family Foundation for the generous grant that made this book possible. We thank Jack Roripaugh and June Roripaugh Tull for the use of their personal photograph collections. We thank Judy Hancock and Pat Hall for allowing us to include photographs of early Temecula from the Horace and Leverne Parker Collection. We thank James Vail "Sandy" Wilkinson for the use of his photographs and for his many hours of interviews. We thank the Knott family and the Barnetts for sharing photographs and information. We thank Peggy Goffman, Jim Knight's granddaughter, for sharing photographs of early ranching from the Knight family collection. We thank the Seay family for allowing us to print his unique photographs of Erle Stanley Gardner and of the Wolf Valley. The photographs of daily life on the Vail Ranch are thanks to Edward G. Polley's generous donation. We thank Robert Roripaugh for his photographs of Vail Ranch operations and his hours of describing machinery and processing of grain on the ranch. We appreciate Jim Ramsay's donation of photographs depicting work on the Vail Ranch. We thank Maryolive Cobb Shoupe for her donation of the family photograph from the Culver family collection. We thank Steven Allen, who scanned the images and put them into a publishable format. And finally, we thank Malcolm Barnett, Darell Farnbach, and Dick Fox for proofreading the manuscript.

One may ask why other families and places are not featured in this book. The answer is that we used the photographs we had access to. If you would like to share photographs with us for a future publication, please contact Loretta Barnett at (951) 676-7031 or Rebecca Farnbach at (951) 699-5148.

INTRODUCTION

The story of Temecula, named by the first inhabitants and translated as "where the sun shines through the mist," can be summarized in telling the tale of three town sites. Unlike Charles Dickens's *Tale of Two Cities* describing two separate burghs, Temecula's story is one continuous tale told in three separate scenes, with an emerging fourth.

Until the first Spanish padres stumbled into the Temecula Valley in 1797, natives lived in the first Temecula, as their ancestors also lived, as hunters and gatherers. They built tule reed and willow structures on the verdant land near the Temecula Creek, where each successive generation heard the stories of their people in songs sung by their elders.

The padres represented Spain. They claimed Temecula's rich pasturelands and the souls dwelling on the land for the church and for Spain. Perhaps well meaning, the padres instructed the natives in European culture and religion, but as a result, life as the natives had known it changed forever.

In the 1830s, when this area was under Mexican rule, a capable Mission Indian named Pablo Apis received the Little Temecula Rancho along the Temecula Creek as a Mexican land grant. This, the tiniest of all the land grants in the valley, sat strategically at the crossroads of the trails leading from east to west and from north to south. Apis sold provisions and lodging to travelers and was privy to news from each direction.

The Butterfield Stage went through the Little Temecula Rancho, and other stagecoaches carried mail and people into the valley. Soon the area boasted several domiciles. Investors bought the nearby Pauba, Temecula, and Santa Rosa Ranchos. The newcomers insisted on dominating the land and in 1874, they waged and won a legal dispute to remove the Temecula Indians, who they considered squatters. Uprooted, the natives settled along the Pechanga Creek.

Louis Wolf, a European emigrant, acquired an adobe general store on the north banks of the Temecula Creek and most of the Little Temecula Rancho. The "King of Temecula," as the Temecula Indians called him, ruled the second Temecula at his Wolf Store. Wolf served as postmaster, merchant, road commissioner, schoolmaster, and justice of the peace. He schemed grand designs to build "Louisville," a town of subdivided lots and homes, but the project was not to take root for nearly 100 years by another's hands and by another name.

The 1882 arrival of the railroad along the foothills near Murrieta Creek prompted commercial growth near the train station, creating the third Temecula, now referred to as Old Town. Wolf built a new store in Old Town, partnering with Macedonia "Mac" Machado, and Hugh McConville built a livery station. Granite from the hills south of town was quarried and shipped by rail to Riverside, Los Angeles, and San Francisco. The Escallier family planted grapes at their home on Main Street and stored their wine in the stone cellar of their barn.

The site of the Wolf Store remained an important site as the new town, called Old Town, grew. In 1905, when Walter Vail added the four local ranchos to his five-state real estate portfolio, he developed the Wolf Store site into the headquarters of operation for his Southern California cattle ranch, while Old Town served as the commercial center.

In 1965, the Vail family sold the ranch to a development company that designed a planned community, named Rancho California instead of Louisville. As subdivisions and businesses grew in the burgeoning city, the Wolf Store and the Vail Ranch headquarters buildings sat empty and forgotten on the open land along Highway 79 South.

Now in the 21st century, the Pechanga Band of Mission Indians welcomes people from all over Southern California to its casino. A Wal-Mart store of general merchandise, a postal annex, and a law office open their doors to the morning sunshine a few paces away from the old Wolf Store. Old Town Temecula retains a rustic charm with antique stores and occasional reenactments of gunfights on the street. Over 20 vineyards attract tourists to their wineries, and a non-profit Vail Ranch Restoration Association works to restore the Vail Ranch Headquarters and Wolf Store into a historical community park.

Coming full circle, the first, second, and third Temeculas are reborn. This book will acquaint the reader with images of bygone days and will help identify traces of the past that remain.

One

RESIDENTS OF THE
FIRST TEMECULA

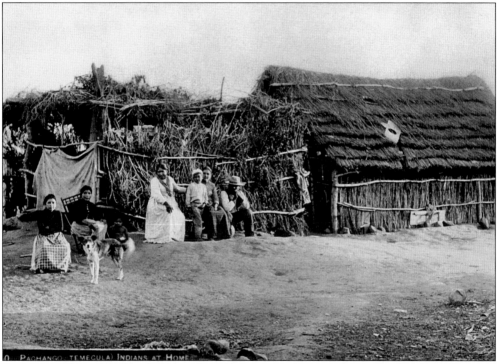

PECHANGA HOME. Before the Spanish padres came to the area, the natives lived in *kishas* near water sources. The ancestors of the Pechanga band of Luiseño Indians lived along the Temecula Creek and were called the Temecula Indians. Their *kishas* resembled pit houses, dug several feet deep with roofs constructed from a framework of branches covered with tule reeds and grass. The Temecula Indians, evicted from their village along the Temecula Creek in 1875, moved to land along the Pechanga Creek. Pechanga, in their language, means "dripping," indicating a spring of water. This photograph represents a typical above ground home of the Pechanga band of Luiseño Indians during the first part of the 1900s. They are called Luiseño because of the influence of the San Luis Rey Mission. Although the tribal name has been spelled several ways in the past, Pechanga is the preferred current spelling. (Courtesy of Horace and Leverne Parker Collection.)

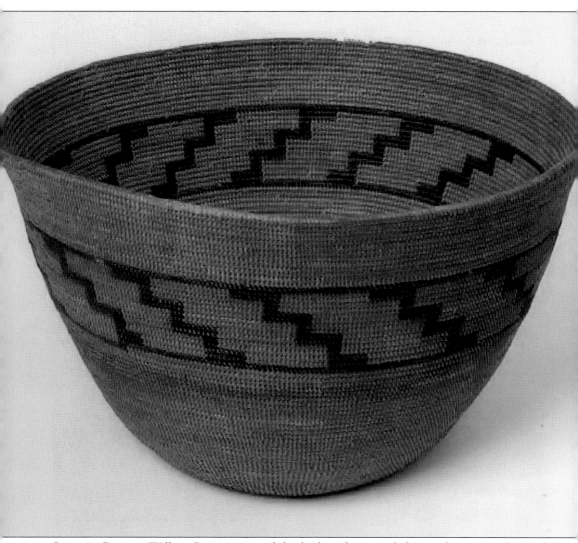

LUISEÑO BASKET. William Banning owned this basket of grass coiled around a sumac splint and decorated with juncus designs. It is representative of a Mission Indian style and is thought to be from the 1800s and Luiseño in origin. The coiling is done in a clockwise direction with ends tucked under. Additional binding stitches finish the rim. The black stitching in the bowl is a flaw woven into the basket "to let the spirit out." The black dyes were often made from boiling twigs of sumac in water with black oxide of iron and black muck from a marsh. Luiseño patterns seldom feature images of living things and are usually distinctively dark on light geometric patterns, many resembling lightning. Women wove baskets from trinket size to large granary sizes for trade or for collecting and storing food. (Courtesy of Museum of the American West, Autry National Center.)

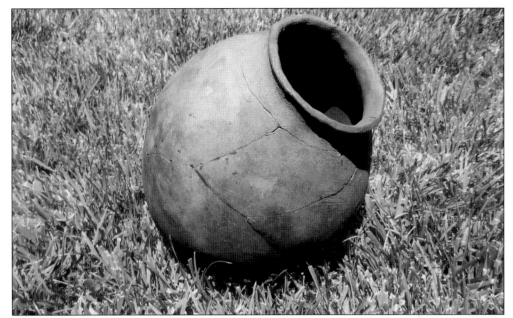

POTTERY. A Temecula Indian woman formed this *olla*, or clay pot, nearly 200 years ago, probably using the broken bottom of another *olla* to shape it. The maker sculpted the local clay with her hands and smoothed it with a piece from a broken pot before pinching off the mouth edge and firing it over the coals of dried cow dung. *Ollas* with small openings stored seeds and kept water cool. This wide-mouth *olla*, found on the Vail Ranch in the early 1900s, shows discoloration from cooking fires. Typically an *olla* like this was used to cook *weewish*, or acorn mush. (Courtesy of VaRRA.)

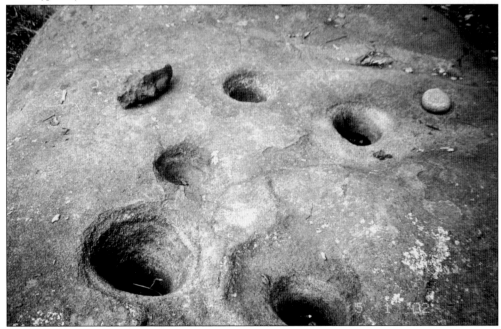

BEDROCK MORTARS. These grinding holes in the granite of Murrieta hills show evidence of crushing or grinding of acorns from nearby trees. Women spent hours crushing and pulverizing acorns and seeds with rocks called *manos*. (Courtesy of Barnett collection.)

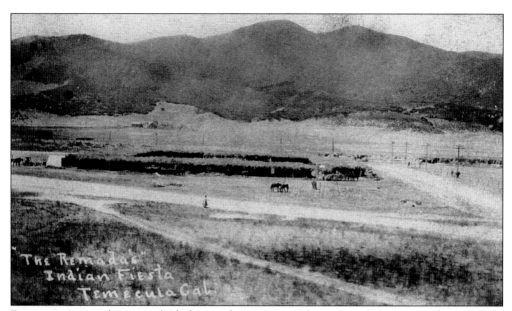

RAMADA. A ramada is a crude shelter used as temporary housing or for a fiesta gathering. Early fiestas were celebrations of hospitality between tribal clans, but after the arrival of the Spanish padres, they evolved into community celebrations. This ramada was built for an annual fiesta. This view shows the hills west of Old Town Temecula. The brush sheds formed a courtyard about 150 square feet. (Courtesy of Barnett collection.)

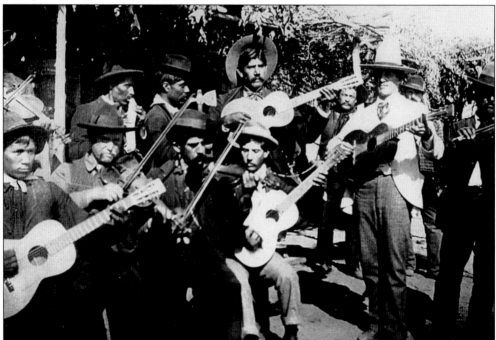

MUSICIANS. Fiddles and guitars supplied music for singing and dancing during fiestas. Music was an important aspect of the early fiestas when local Indians sang songs about their enemies and danced the whirling dance, the feather dance, and the war dance. Later groups like this provided music for ballroom dancing, which lasted all night. (Courtesy of Barnett collection.)

FIESTA. Maude Van Nest wrote on this card postmarked 1908 that she had been to the fiesta near Temecula. Two men with a watering can and pail are shown preparing the ramada for the traditional three-day festivities. The poster reads, "Tonight grand entertainment by the Mexican Acrobatic Troupe, Admission 25 cents." (Courtesy of Barnett collection.)

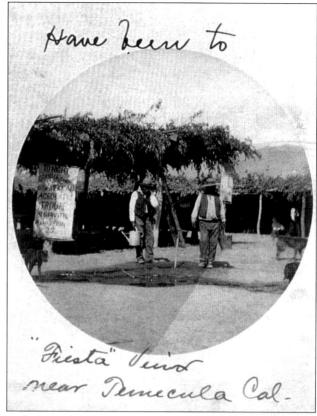

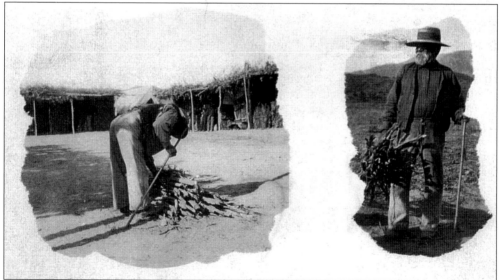

INSIDE AND OUTSIDE THE RAMADA. A worker sets down a large bundle of wood in the center of the ramada, while several other men watch from the shaded background. The roofs of the ramada are covered with thick green branches to provide cool shade for the heat of the day. Outside the man supports himself with a stick as he carries his load to the ramada. His hat and sleeves keep the bright sun from burning his skin. (Courtesy of Barnett collection.)

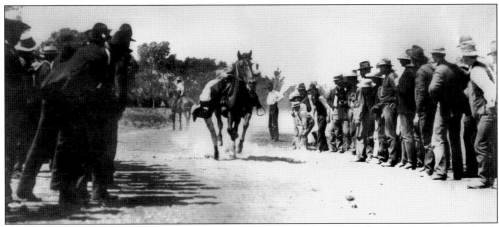

ROOSTER PULL. This sport challenged men's bravado and riding skills. A rider on horseback would reach down to pull the head off a rooster buried to its neck in the ground. Between 1910 and 1920, rooster pulls were held on the grounds of what is now Sam Hicks Monument in front of the Temecula Valley Museum. In later years, a more humane game of spearing potatoes from the ground replaced the rooster pull. (Courtesy of Horace and Leverne Parker Collection.)

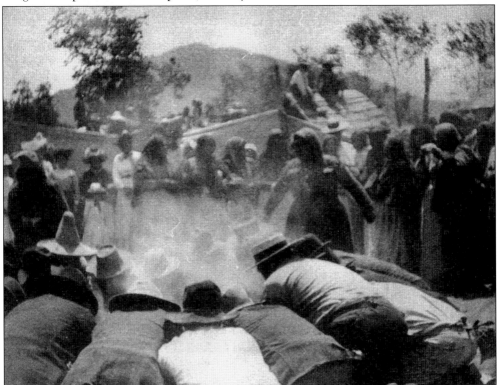

PEON GAME. In this game, two opposing teams of four men held *peones*, the wrist bones of coyotes, in their clenched fists. The teams sat across from each other and kept their hands under a blanket, holding the edges of the blanket in their teeth. Each man had one white and one black *peon*. Bets were placed on which color *peon* was in a hand. The game sometimes lasted a week, and Agua Caliente Indians were known to have returned to their homes in Palm Springs to get more betting money. (Courtesy of Horace and Leverne Parker Collection.)

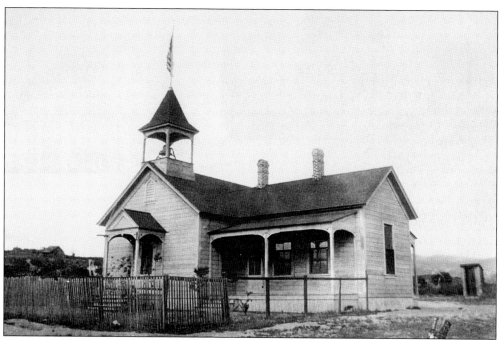

PECHANGA SCHOOL. This 1898 photograph shows the Pechanga Reservation School. The first school, constructed from adobe and wood, blew down in a windstorm and was replaced with a wooden structure that was demolished by fire in 1891. The third school burned in 1894 under suspicious circumstances, cremating the teacher inside. (Courtesy of Horace and Leverne Parker Collection.)

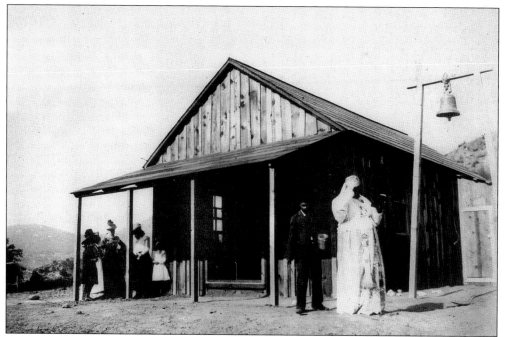

PECHANGA CHURCH. A priest blesses the bells at St. Gabriel's Church, located about a mile inside the Pechanga Reservation. (Courtesy of Horace and Leverne Parker Collection.)

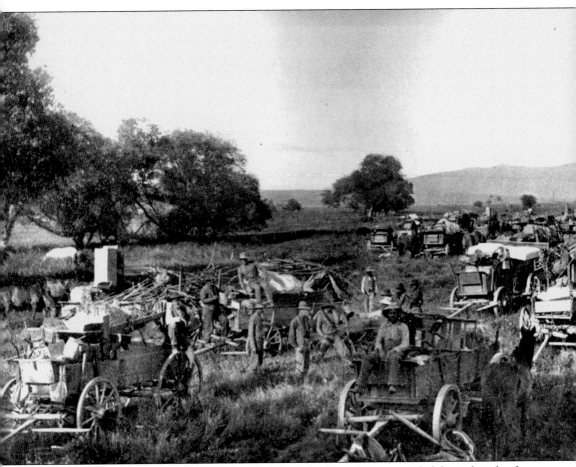

EXILES CAMPING AT PAUBA RANCH. In 1903, the Cupa Indians, exiled from their lands near Warner Ranch, followed the Old Butterfield Stage Route to the Pauba Ranch, where they camped for the night. Local ranchers offered their wagons to carry their belongings. The 39-mile, three-day "Trail of Tears" ended in the Pala Valley, where they lived in tents until more durable structures were erected. In 2003, over 200 descendants of the original Cupa families traced the route of their ancestors in reverse and for three days rented 41 cottages, including the 17 original adobes their families once owned. They celebrated a fiesta with singing and dancing. On their return to Pala, several ran the 39 miles in a relay. (Courtesy of VaRRA.)

Two

THE SECOND
TEMECULA

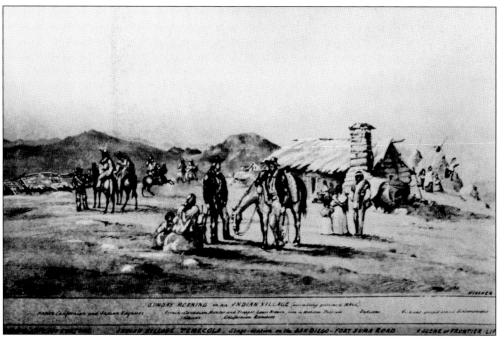

APIS'S ADOBE. This drawing, the Vischer Sketch, looking westward in 1865, shows the adobe house of Pablo Apis on the Little Temecula Rancho and the Indian village of Temecula in the background. Apis, an Indian born at Rancho Guajome near the present-day town of Vista, was educated at Mission San Luis Rey, where he distinguished himself as a capable leader. Although it was unusual for an Indian to receive a Mexican land grant, Apis was given the Little Temecula Rancho. Travelers along the Fort Yuma Road, which later became the Butterfield Stage Route, recalled his ranch as a place of repose and good food along the way of their journeys. It is believed to be the place where an Indian treaty was signed in 1852. (Courtesy of VaRRA.)

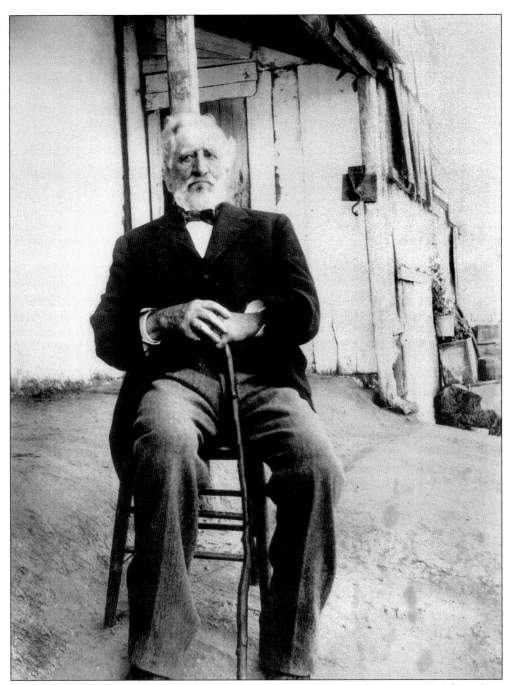

JOHN MAGEE, 1826–1901. This photograph was taken at Magee's home near Rainbow Gap, shortly before he died. Considered Temecula's first merchant, Magee ran a general store along the Old Butterfield Stage Route on the south side of the Temecula Creek, about a quarter mile from where the Wolf Store is today. He later moved to the location pictured on the road to San Diego and ran a store there. (Courtesy of Horace and Leverne Parker Collection.)

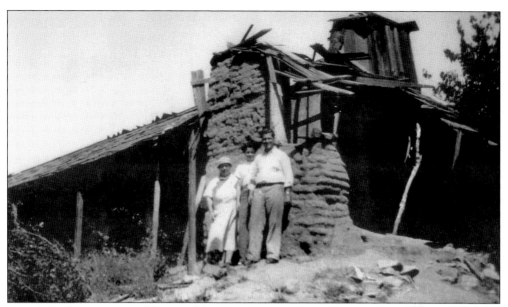

AUGUSTA, LEVERNE, AND HORACE PARKER AT MAGEE STORE RUINS, 1934. The second Magee Store was in poor condition when local historian Horace Parker visited it with his mother and future wife. Horace, son of the Temecula depot agent, grew up in Temecula and went to high school in Elsinore before becoming a veterinarian. He was living on Balboa Island in the 1960s when he decided to buy burial plots in Temecula and learned he could not buy one unless he owned property in the town. To meet the requirements, he bought the old Temecula Hotel property and refurbished it to make a residence. His wife, Leverne, continued to make the old hotel her home for many years, while Horace rested in the Temecula Public Cemetery. While he was alive, Horace conducted interviews of old-timers and published Temecula's history in three booklets. He also wrote a newspaper column called the Brush Country Journal. Horace and Leverne archived artifacts, documents, and photographs. Leverne was a talented artist who painted scenes of Temecula and mission chapels. (Courtesy of Horace and Leverne Parker Collection.)

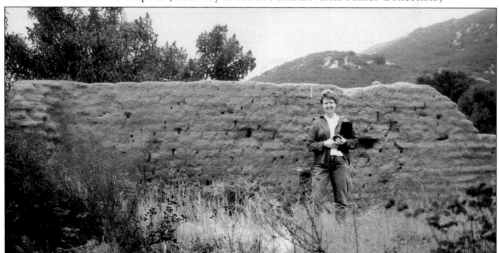

MAGEE STORE RUINS, 2001. Local historian Rebecca Farnbach poses beside one of the three partial adobe walls still standing on property owned by the Pechanga band of Luiseño Indians. The tribe plans to protect the walls from further deterioration. (Courtesy of VaRRA.)

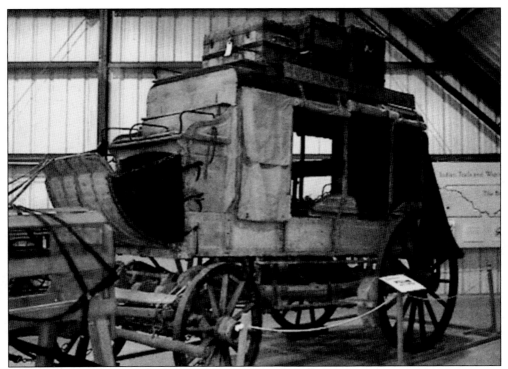

MUD WAGON. The Overland Butterfield Stage Company ran this model of stagecoach to Temecula during the short time the company carried mail and passengers west from St. Louis (1858–1861). It cost $150 for a one-way ticket for the three-week trip from St. Louis to San Francisco. The route followed the Old Emigrant Trail, the only all-year route to California, coming from Yuma to Warner Springs and through Oak Grove to Temecula. This stagecoach is displayed in the Gilman Historic Ranch and Wagon Museum in Banning. (Courtesy of VaRRA.)

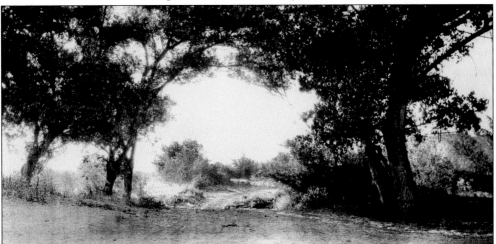

RIVER CROSSING. Because of quicksand and marshlands, few places along the Temecula Creek allowed crossing before the construction of a bridge on Pala Road and much later on Redhawk Parkway. This historical river crossing of the Old Emigrant Trail followed by the Overland Butterfield Stage Company and other travelers is located east of the Redhawk Parkway Bridge. (Courtesy of Sandy Wilkinson.)

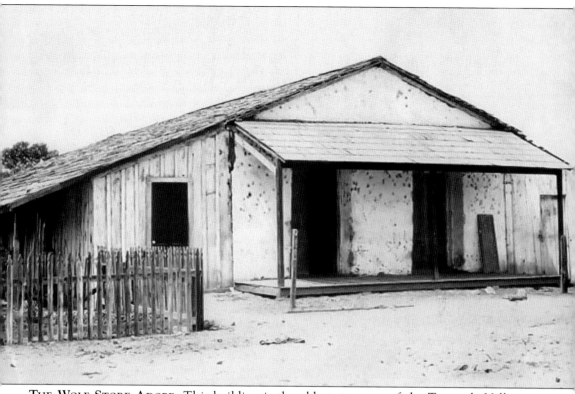

THE WOLF STORE ADOBE. This building is the oldest structure of the Temecula Valley. It is unknown who built it, although some speculate Louis Wolf or John Magee was responsible. The adobe was first mentioned in letters around 1867. It housed a general store, a stage stop, law office, hotel, and post office. Although it bustled as the center of commerce and politics from 1867 through the 1890s, it was used for grain storage during the Vail Ranch era of 1905 through 1964. (Courtesy of Autry National Center and Southwest Museum of the American Indian.)

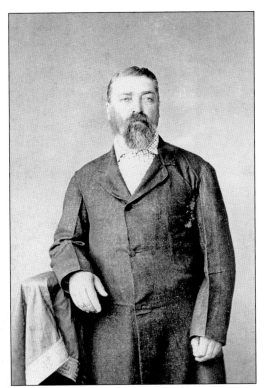

LOUIS WOLF, 1833–1887. This Jewish native of Alsace-Lorraine, on the fluctuating border between France and Germany, was an entrepreneur who built a thriving business in the adobe store that carries his name on the north side of the Temecula Creek. Wolf was the storekeeper, postmaster, justice of peace, road commissioner, and school board trustee. Temecula Indians called him the King of Temecula. (Courtesy of San Diego Historical Society.)

RAMONA PLACE WOLF, 1846–1894. Ramona Wolf was born in Santa Barbara to a whaling ship cook from the West Indies and an Indian woman. The famous author Helen Hunt Jackson stayed with Louis and Ramona Wolf and immortalized them as the keepers of Hartzell's Store in her novel *Ramona*, which depicted the tragedy of the Indians living among the California ranchers during the late 1800s. (Courtesy of San Diego Historical Society.)

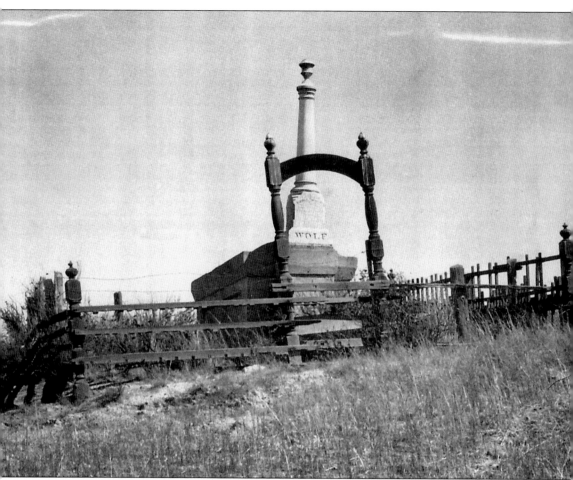

THE WOLF MONUMENT. This monument pays tribute to Louis Wolf, one of the most influential of the early Temecula settlers, and three of his children who preceded him to the grave. When he died, the *San Diego Union* newspaper said, "Wolf, one of the oldest residents of San Diego County died at his residence in Temecula where he began a trading post with Indians in a small adobe store in 1859 with only brawn, brain, industry and perseverance as capital, but amassed a snug fortune." For several decades, the monument suffered neglect until the Temecula Historical Society undertook a restoration project in 2001, restored its foundation, and replaced the marble column that had been kept safe at a private residence. His wife, Ramona, was buried at the Mission San Luis Rey. Temecula was part of San Diego County until Riverside County was formed in 1893. (Courtesy of Horace and Leverne Parker Collection.)

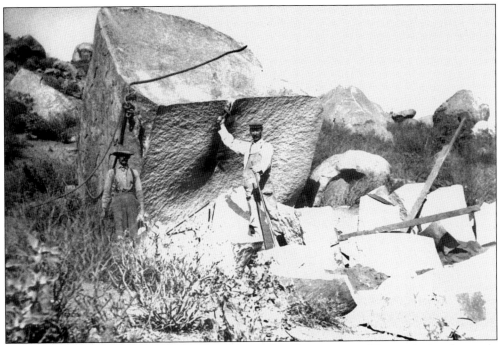

TEMECULA GRANITE QUARRY. When the railroad came into Temecula in the early 1880s opening a way to transport granite quarried from the hills south of Temecula, a new industry began. The rock was already used locally for hitching posts, grave markers, and for foundations of houses. Workers took wagons holding five tons of granite to the train station three times a day to load on flatcars bound for Riverside, Los Angeles, and San Francisco. (Courtesy of Barnett collection.)

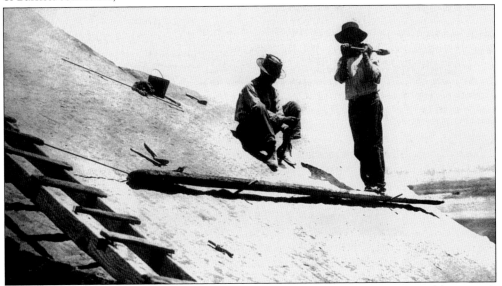

DRILLING GRANITE. The granite was easily accessible because it lay on the surface of the ground, but the immensity made it impossible to manage without cutting it into smaller pieces. Black powder explosive charges were set into lines of holes dug into the rock by star-shaped drills. The force split the rocks from the hillside. (Courtesy of Barnett collection.)

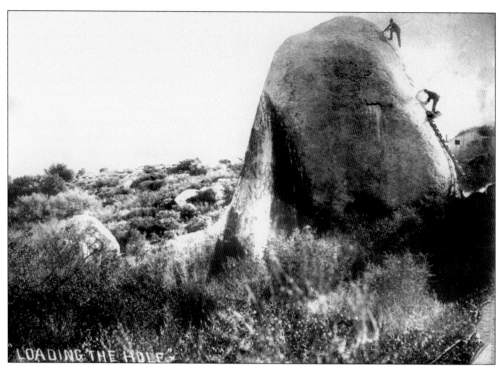

LOADING THE HOLE. Two men loaded holes with black powder to blast the granite from the hillside in one of the over 20 quarries that once extracted rock from the hills above Wolf Valley and Rainbow Canyon. (Courtesy of Barnett collection.)

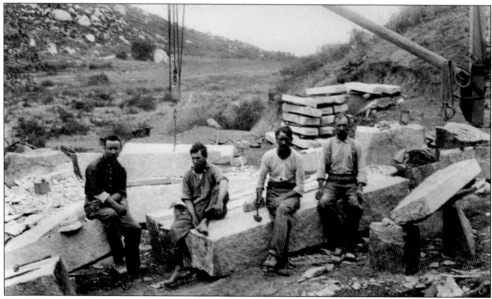

GRANITE WORKERS ON BOULDERS. Large quantities of Temecula granite were shipped to use for street curbs, steps, and foundations of buildings in Riverside, Los Angeles, and San Francisco until the popularity of concrete rendered the business obsolete. The portability and ease of shaping concrete, coupled with reduction of shipping costs, heralded the close of the Temecula quarries in the 1920s. (Courtesy of VaRRA.)

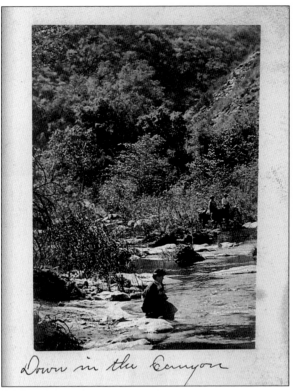

DOWN IN THE CANYON. This 1907 postcard carries a message from Maude Van Nest, who married Ormiston Gonzalez. A gentleman angler casts his hopes in the background as two men on horseback watch. Van Nest is dressed formally compared to today's typical fishing attire, wearing her hat, cape, and skirt. (Courtesy of Barnett collection.)

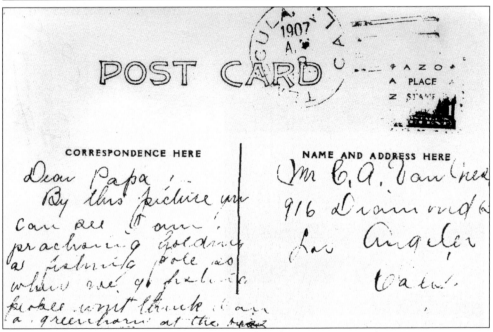

POSTCARD TEXT. The reverse of Maude's postcard reads, "Dear Papa, By this picture you can see I am practicing holding a fishing pole so when we go fishing people won't think I'm a greenhorn at the sport." The card went to C. A. Van Nest on Diamond Avenue in Los Angles. (Courtesy of Barnett collection.)

TEMECULA CANYON. A young man and two young ladies stand on a path above the Margarita River west of the confluence of the Temecula and Murrieta Creeks. This canyon provides the cool ocean breeze that is responsible for the mild climate of the Temecula Valley. Vineyards thrive in the nearby wine country because of the afternoon breeze that prevents the grapes from overheating in the hot summer sunshine. (Courtesy of VaRRA.)

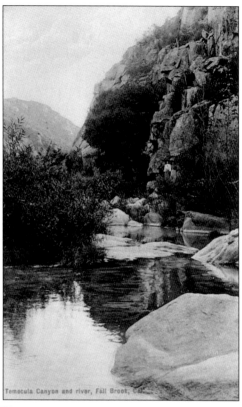

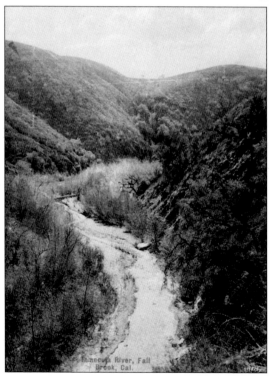

OVERVIEW OF TEMECULA CANYON. The remnants of a railroad trestle are visible in this postcard photograph. This and the postcard above were both printed in Germany by M. Rieder of Los Angeles for Miss A. M. Carpenter of "Fall Brook, Cal." It was postmarked 1910. (Courtesy of VaRRA.)

27

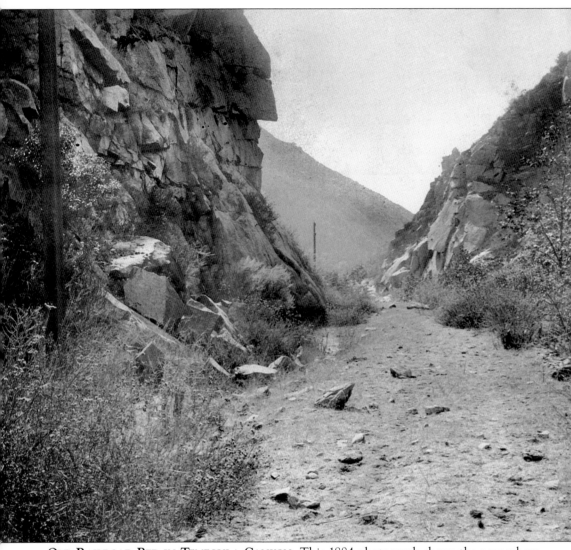

OLD RAILROAD BED IN TEMECULA CANYON. This 1884 photograph shows the area where the California Southern Railroad tracks were washed out during rainstorms earlier that year. Constructed in 1882, the ill-fated rail route gave faster service than wagon or stagecoach between National City and Colton for a $9 round-trip cost. During the heavy rainfall of the storm, the passengers hiked three miles to get out of the canyon. The Wells Fargo agent stayed to guard the train. When the agent saw the train was doomed, he built a raft and went down river. The tracks were rebuilt along the same route because it was thought the flood was a once in a 100-year event. In 1891, the tracks washed out again and were never rebuilt. (Courtesy of Barnett collection.)

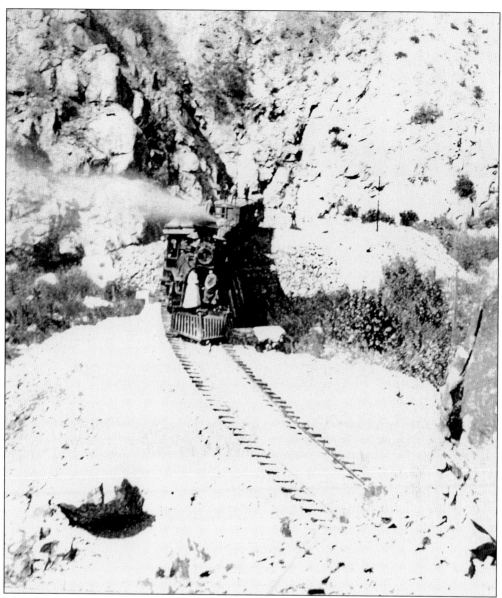

THE CALIFORNIA SOUTHERN RAILROAD. After the tracks were washed out in the Temecula Canyon in 1891, the line ceased running between Temecula and National City, but continued to run from Temecula to Colton until 1935. The line shipped passengers and goods into Temecula and carried granite, potatoes, and cattle out. The Vail Company had cattle-holding pens and the warehouse to keep produce and grain near the tracks. (Courtesy of Horace and Leverne Parker Collection.)

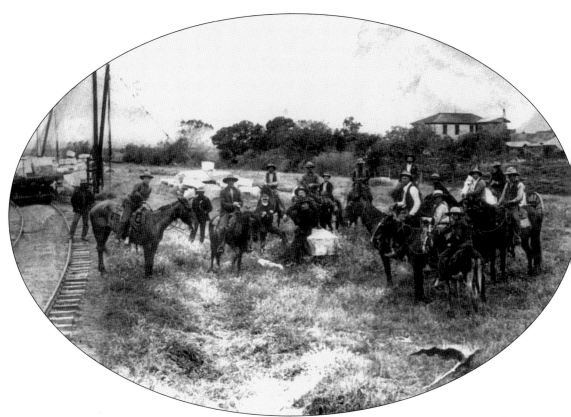

COWBOYS BY TRAIN TRACKS. This photograph shows cowboys by the Temecula tracks west of the Murrieta Creek just south of town. The flatcar at the left is still loaded with granite blocks from a quarry farther south along the tracks. Cowboys would ride in from the Pauba Ranch on a Saturday night to have a good time and a few drinks. Sometimes the ranch foreman would have to spend Sunday morning collecting a cowboy from the sheriff's custody. (Courtesy of Barnett collection.)

Three

EARLY DAYS IN OLD TOWN TEMECULA

JOE WINKLES, 1879–1939. Temecula's most colorful figure was Joe Winkles, who came to town in 1902 when a Los Angeles employment agency secured a position for him at Hugh McConville's Palace Livery. Winkles is shown here riding a mule and draped with a flag during a Fourth of July parade. The photograph is taken looking northwest between the Burnham Mercantile Store and E. E. Barnett's Store, which advertised sales of furnishings, farm implements, and general merchandise. Winkles bought the Welty Building and renamed it Ramona Inn. At first glance, only the legitimate business of card tables and rooms for rent was visible, but the Ramona Inn had slot machines and was known throughout Southern California as a "Blind Pig Saloon," a place that sold liquor illegally during Prohibition. His illegitimate business attracted the Hollywood crowd and boxing champions to Temecula. His well-known customers parked their cars behind the inn so they could come and go undetected. Winkles also invested in the First National Bank and in granite quarries. (Courtesy of Knott family.)

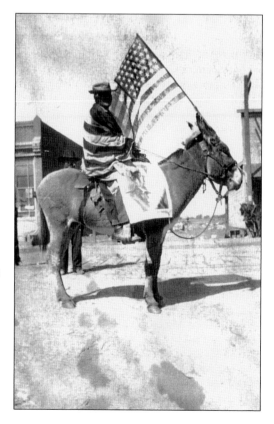

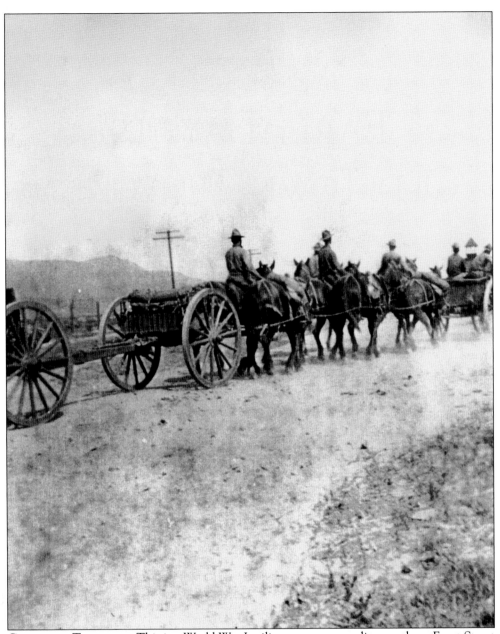

CONVOY IN TEMECULA. This is a World War I military convoy traveling north on Front Street from San Diego through Temecula. The steeple in the background is the Catholic church. A Elsinore newspaper article on July 11, 1919, about Temecula reads, "what would our heroes who fought for us in the world war think if we did not show them that we were overjoyed to see them return to their homes and to their mothers who were anxiously counting the days for their return. We are not slackers and do not care to be called slackers because our little town, in proportion, furnished Uncle Sam as many soldiers as any city in the United States, and it must be remembered that our subscription to Liberty bonds was more than three times our quota for the third Liberty bond issue. Our quota was $11,000 and our subscription was $77,000. Just think, seven times over. Isn't that going over the top? Can you beat that?" (Courtesy of Knott family.)

OLE LARSON, 1886–1966. Ole Larson, shown here on Front Street about 1906, is decked out in a shirt and tie with his striped bib overalls. His mare Babe is also dressed for the occasion with silver-trimmed tack featuring a heart on the forehead and chest. Larson enjoyed a variety of careers. For a while, he worked at the livery stable and was responsible for operating the telephone switchboard 24 hours a day, seven days a week. He was a constable, did some ranching, and checked surveying of Indian reservations for the U.S. government. He owned barbershops in Fallbrook, next to the bank in Temecula, and later at Guenther's Murrieta Hot Springs Resort. (Courtesy of Knott family.)

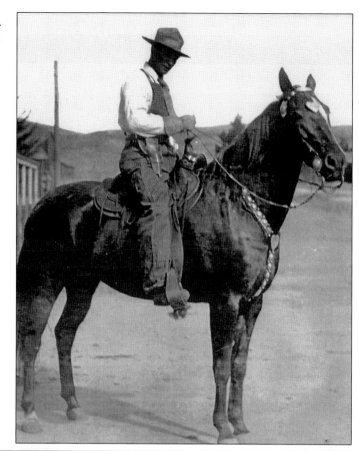

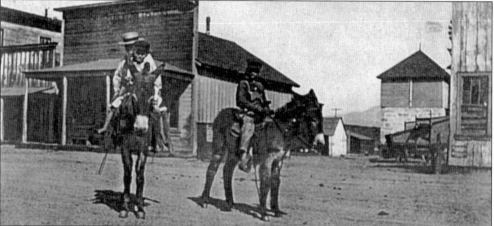

FRANK BURNHAM ON DONKEY. Frank Burnham is riding a donkey on Main Street. His father, George, operated the Burnham Store, now known as the Mercantile Store. Until 1956, Frank ran a general merchandise store in Murrieta. The small two-story building in the right background is often called a jail, but it was originally built as a food and wine cellar with walls made of one-foot thick scrap granite. A water tank sat atop the granite cellar. The windmill next to it pumped water from underground into the tank for storage. The wine cellar was also used for cold storage in days before refrigeration. (Courtesy of Horace and Leverne Parker Collection.)

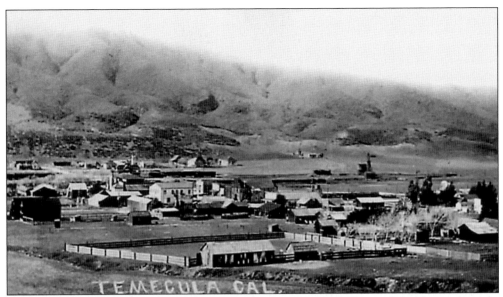

Panorama of Early Temecula, 1909. Fruit trees grace an early Temecula garden in the right foreground of this photograph, looking northwest. The background shows a water tower and windmill to supply water for the train. Also visible are the McConville house and barn, the livery stable, and the Welty Building. (Courtesy of Security Pacific Collection/Los Angeles Public Library.)

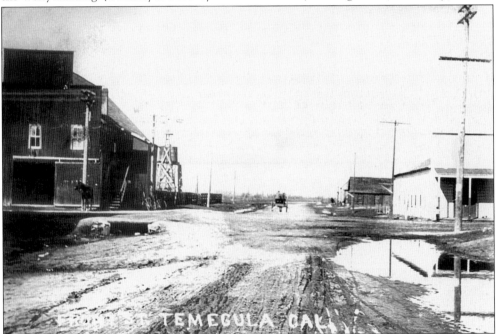

Horse and Cart on Front Street. This gives us a glimpse of the tree-barren town of Temecula in times past, before streets were paved. Muddy in the aftermath of a rainstorm, a lone horse pulls two people in a buggy going north on Front Street past the Palace Livery Stable where another horse is hitched. A boy at the side of the white building watches the buggy. A windmill whirls near the water tower behind the livery station and the sky threatens more rain. (Courtesy of Barnett collection.)

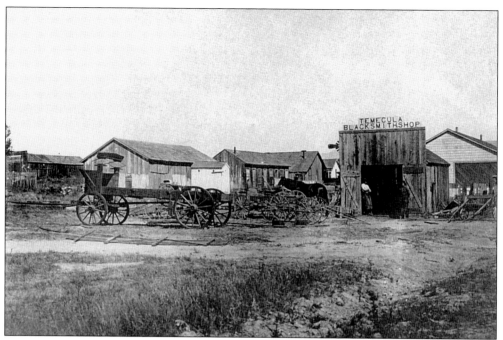

TEMECULA BLACKSMITH SHOP, 1900. This is a view of East Main Street in 1900, when horses and horse-drawn conveyances dominated the roads. A blacksmith was needed, but not an automobile mechanic. Two men pose near the entrance to the shop. (Courtesy of Knott family.)

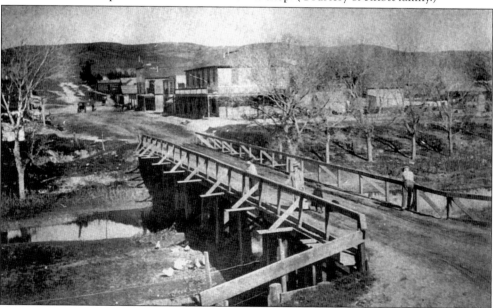

MAIN STREET BRIDGE. While ducks bask in the sunshine below, five people and a dog linger on the bridge over the meager stream of the Murrieta Creek. Looking east on Main Street, a driver is stopped to talk to a man with a dog. The bare trees along the creek bed signify wintertime. The Temecula Hotel, previously the Welty Hotel, is in the center of the picture. Beyond the hotel are the Friedemann Meat Market, originally the H. G. Vogel and North Meat Market, and the Machado Store. (Courtesy of Barnett collection.)

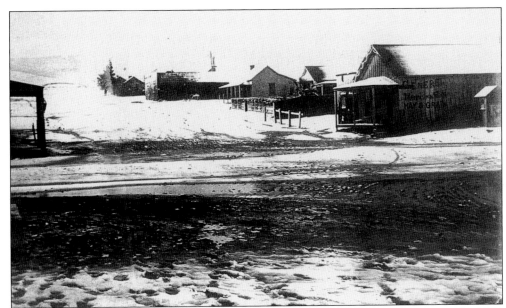

SNOW ON MAIN STREET. This is the corner of Main and Front Streets, looking east. In 1882, Louis Wolf and Macedonia "Mac" Machado were partners in the building on the corner that was later called the Machado Store. In this photograph, the roof sports a rare covering of snow. The store burned down in 1888, destroying all its contents and damaging the adjacent Machado and Wolf homes. The store was rebuilt in 1909 with terra cotta, which was made in the Alberhill brick kilns and covered with stucco. (Courtesy of Barnett collection.)

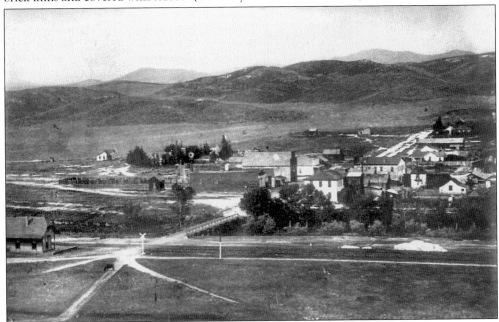

LOOKING EAST THROUGH OLD TOWN TEMECULA. When Wolf and Machado opened their store, it was in the New Town of Temecula, meaning the town had moved from the Wolf Store on the Old Emigrant Trail along Highway 79 South to the third Temecula near the rail lines. This photograph looks west of the train depot to the hills east of the settlement. (Courtesy of Barnett collection.)

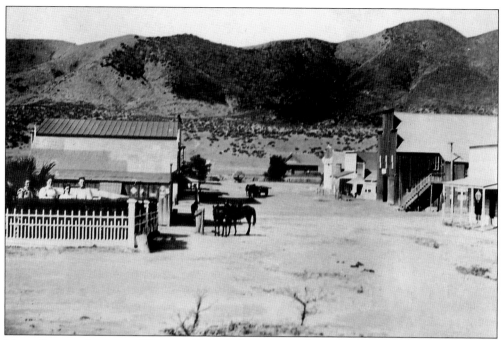

MAIN STREET, LOOKING WEST, C. 1901. Ladies pose in the yard of the Machado home across the street from the Escallier Pool and Billiard Parlor. The Livery Stable and Burnham's General Merchandise Store are visible down the street. (Courtesy of Barnett collection.)

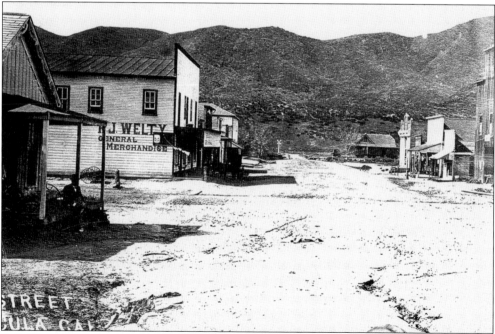

R. J. WELTY GENERAL MERCHANDISE STORE. Looking west on Main Street, the Welty Building is seen. The ground floor of the 1890 building housed a general store, with rooms rented upstairs. Joe Winkles bought this building and entertained the Hollywood crowd at his Blind Pig Saloon. Winkles removed upstairs partitions to make it into a boxing ring. (Courtesy of Barnett collection.)

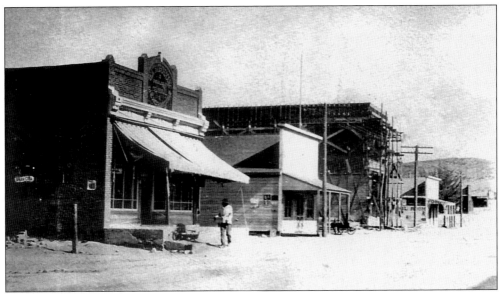

BUILDING THE BANK. In the early days of Temecula, merchants bartered goods for agricultural products or wild game and paid bills for customers, adding the sum to their accounts. As Temecula grew in population and as commercial enterprises required cash, several businessmen decided the town needed a bank where the cash could be kept safe from theft. The promoters, led by E. E. Barnett, sold stock in the bank and in 1913, they bought the land where the livery stable had stood. (Courtesy of Barnett collection.)

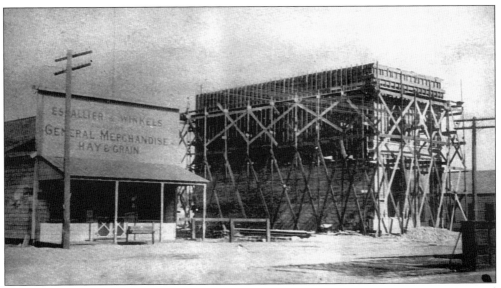

FIRST NATIONAL BANK OF TEMECULA. On June 14, 1914, the two-story concrete First National Bank of Temecula opened. The committee who planned the construction and operations of the bank, which cost over $10,000, were Eli Barnett, C. P. Shumate, Hugo Guenther, George Burnham, Frank Fernald, Alex and Peter Escallier, and Joe Winkles. (Courtesy of Barnett collection.)

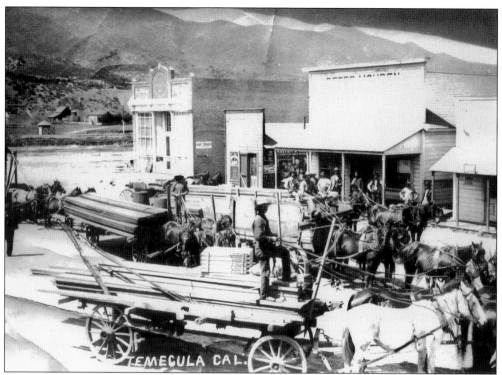

HAULING CONSTRUCTION SUPPLIES. Eli Barnett's sons Mark and Ben stand on wagons loaded with construction supplies, creating one of Temecula's first traffic jams. Across Murrieta Creek, to the left of the Burnham Store, is the McConville house and barn, which are still standing. (Courtesy of Barnett collection.)

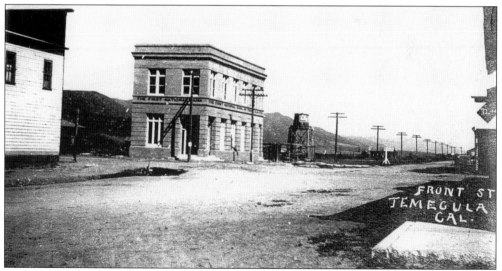

FINISHED BANK. The bank featured a "fine steel Mosler Safe" and ornamental tile floor blocks. Mahlon Vail joined the board of directors and was elected president when the Vail Company bought all but $1,000 of Eli Barnett's shares in 1917. The bank closed in 1943 and reopened as a used bookstore before becoming a Mexican restaurant in 1978. The restaurant is still open today and features several paintings depicting old times in Temecula. (Courtesy of Barnett collection.)

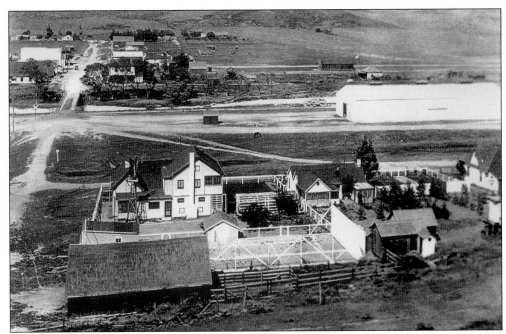

BURNHAM HOUSE. The Burnham home has a windmill in the backyard. George Burnham bought the Mercantile Store (upper left of photograph) from Philip Pohlman, who won the store property in a lottery in 1889 and built it with bricks from an abandoned brickyard. The Burnham family operated the general store until 1953. The 150-by-60-foot fireproof warehouse was constructed in 1915 by J. A. August and E. E. Beatty. The dirt road in front of the homes is the present-day Pujol Street. (Courtesy of Barnett collection.)

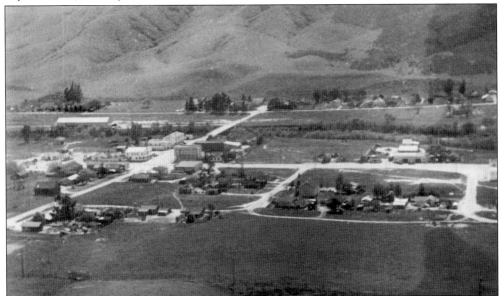

AERIAL VIEW OF TEMECULA, LOOKING WEST. Buildings that can be identified in this photograph include the bank, Mercantile Store, Knott's Garage, Machado Store, Welty Building, and the Temecula Hotel. Also prominent are the Main Street Bridge, the railroad tracks, and the produce warehouse. (Courtesy of Barnett collection.)

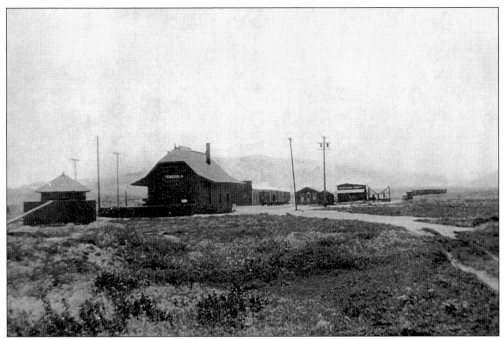

TEMECULA TRAIN DEPOT. Chinese work crews completed the California Southern Railroad line from National City to Temecula through the granite walls of Temecula Canyon. Antonio Ashman recalled riding in his family's spring wagon to watch the construction. He also remembered the thrill of riding the train in 1889 when he was 10 years old. About 100 years later, the Temecula Community Center on Pujol Street was built to resemble the train depot. (Courtesy of Horace and Leverne Parker Collection.)

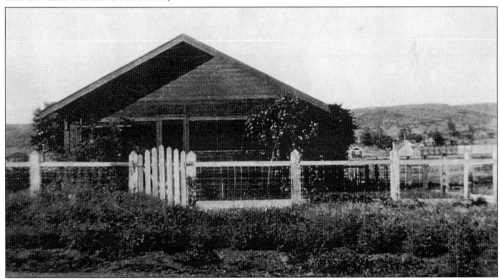

TEMECULA TRAIN DEPOT HOUSE. The train depot house was on Pujol Street. Dr. Horace Parker's father was the last depot agent. As an only child, Horace spent a lot of time at the Barnett Ranch with Ben and Ysabel Barnett's three boys Ralph, Chester, and Francis. Horace came back to Temecula after buying the Temecula Hotel. (Courtesy of Horace and Leverne Parker Collection.)

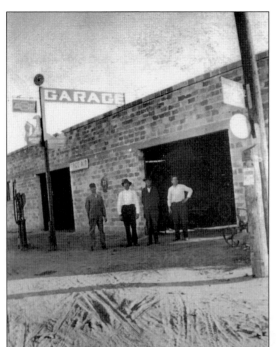

KNOTT'S GARAGE ON UNPAVED STREET. The one grade of gasoline was first pumped into the glass holding area of the lone pump where the quantity was measured before it was drained into the automobile gas tank. Temecula, with a population of about 200 people, did not require any more stations. Not every household owned a car. Ferrell Freeman used to hitch two plow horses to a wagon to get around. Al Knott is the second from the left; the other men are unidentified. (Courtesy of Knott family.)

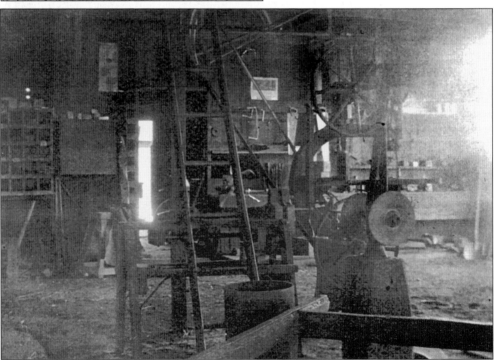

INSIDE AL KNOTT'S BLACKSMITH SHOP, 1957. Al Knott started as the town blacksmith and learned to be an automobile mechanic when demand for the service grew. He continued blacksmithing long after it was a lost art. He shoed horses, repaired wagon wheels, and sharpened mowing machines. This inside view of his blacksmith shop shows old tools, a grinding wheel, pulleys, and a wagon wheel that he made. (Courtesy of Knott family.)

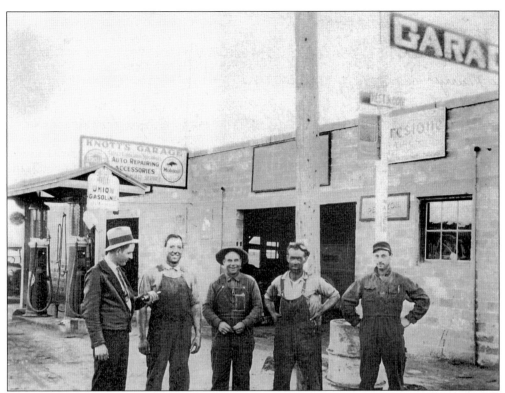

MEN IN FRONT OF KNOTT'S GARAGE. Al Knott was first a blacksmith, then owned an automobile repair business. As a young man, Knott worked for Ferrell Freeman in the Temecula Iron Works, a blacksmith shop located at Front Street and Fifth Street. In 1908, Freeman offered to let Knott buy the business over time, making payments whenever Knott had a few dollars saved. Knott eventually bought 10 lots across the street. The blacksmith building was put on dollies and rolled across Front Street to its second location. These five men are an unidentified salesman from Riverside, Al Knott, Charley Carstensen, Ray Murray, and Carlo Nielson. Signs indicate the "lubrication specialist" used Mobiloil, Penzoil, and Union Gasoline. He also sold Firestone tires. (Courtesy of Knott family.)

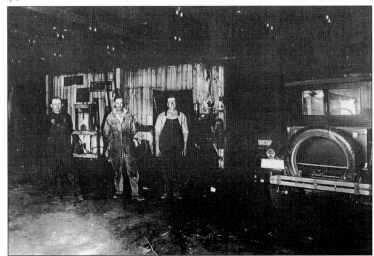

INSIDE AL KNOTT'S GARAGE, AFTER 1918. Art Ramsdale, Carlo Neilson, and Al Knott pose inside the garage with a car. Knott opened the garage in 1918. It was the social gathering place of Temecula. In 1968, he closed his business. (Courtesy of Knott family.)

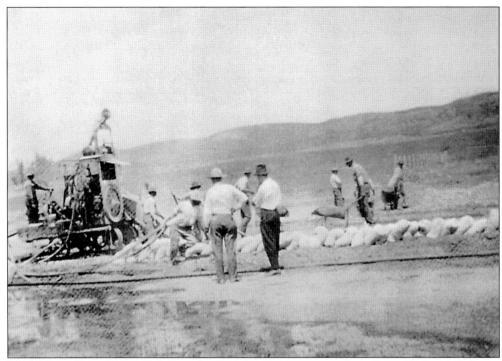

SURFACING FRONT STREET, 1916. In 1916, Front Street, once busy State Highway 395, was surfaced. The workers used wheelbarrows and machinery to make and spread the cement that hardened to form a solid driving surface. (Courtesy of Knott family.)

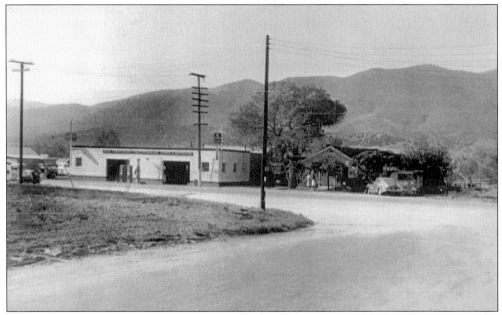

KNOTT'S GARAGE AND HOME. Al Knott walked next door to get to work, unlike many of the residents of present-day Temecula, who commute to Los Angeles or San Diego. This photograph shows three gas pumps at the station that has been painted white. The sign advertises oil, lubrication, tires, and batteries. (Courtesy of Knott family.)

VERA AND VERNON KNOTT, WALKING SOUTH ON FRONT STREET. The Knott twins were born to Al and Freda Knott in 1916. They graduated from Temecula Grammar School and Elsinore Union High School. The brown structure in the background is the Catholic church. The twins remained close all their lives. (Courtesy of Knott family.)

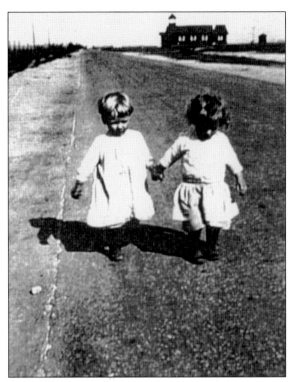

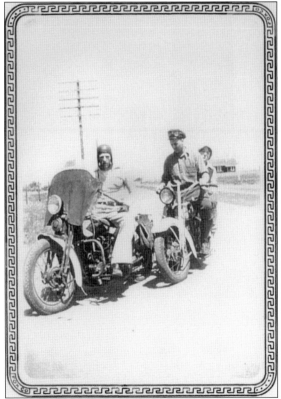

VERA, VERNON, AND ELDON KNOTT. This photograph was taken at nearly the same place on Front Street as the photograph of the twins above. The brown Catholic church is in the background. (Courtesy of Knott family.)

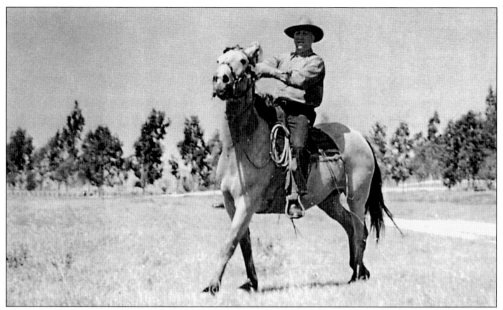

AL KNOTT ON HORSEBACK. Al Knott is riding his horse Flossie in this photograph taken by Sam Hicks. Al loved horses and belonged to a Murrieta riding group. His skills at blacksmithing and horseshoeing were known throughout the valley. (Courtesy of Knott family.)

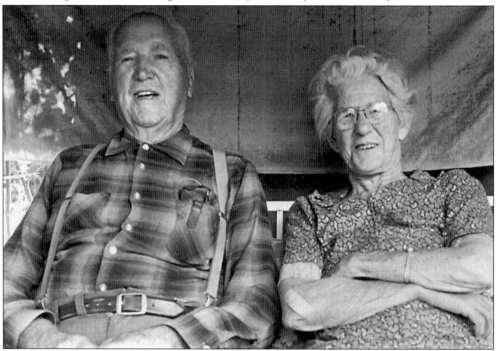

AL KNOTT AND FREDA KNOTT, AFTER RETIREMENT. Al Knott and Freda Rail were married in April 1914. The Rails were a pioneer family of Murrieta. Al owned and operated the blacksmith shop, garage, and gas station on Front Street before he retired. Freda was a Sunday school teacher at the Community Church, which was called "Mrs. Knott's Church," for 60 years. When the Knotts retired in 1965, they moved to Rainbow, California. (Courtesy of Knott family.)

Four

FAMILIES OF THE
THIRD TEMECULA

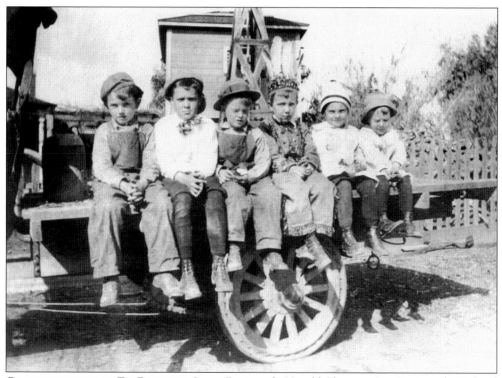

GRANDCHILDREN OF ELI BARNETT. Louie Roripaugh, Harold Clogston, Leo Roripaugh, Richard Barnett, Dorothy Clogston, and Helen Clogston, all grandchildren of Eli or E. E. Barnett, pose on a wagon. Louie became the foreman of the Vail Ranch, Leo was a rancher, and Richard was a farmer. All of the Clogstons moved away. (Courtesy of Barnett collection.)

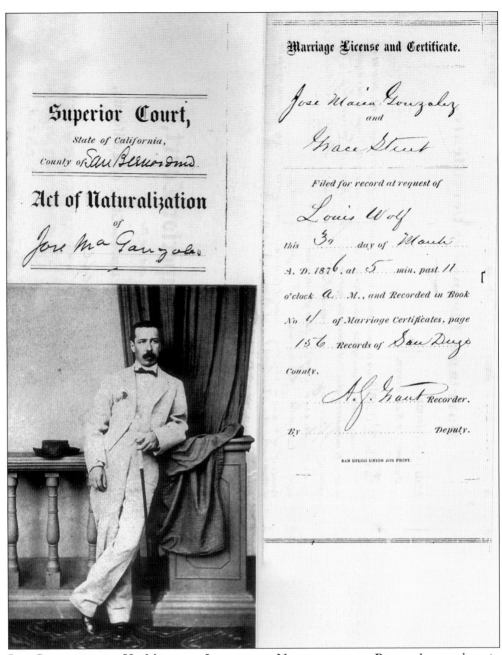

JOSE GONZALEZ WITH HIS MARRIAGE LICENSE AND NATURALIZATION PAPERS. Jose was born in Cadiz, Spain, in 1835 and arrived in San Francisco in the early 1870s. John Magee, justice of the peace, united Jose in marriage with Grace Street at the Temecula Ranch on March 3, 1876, with Juan Murrieta and Isidor Loeb as witnesses. The marriage was recorded at the request of Louis Wolf. On September 27, 1881, Jose became a citizen of the United States. He was an accountant and managed business affairs for investment partners Juan and Ezequiel Murrieta, Domingo Pujol, and Francisco Sanjurjo, who owned the Temecula and Pauba Ranchos and other land, including San Simeon and lands in San Luis Obispo County. (Courtesy of Barnett collection.)

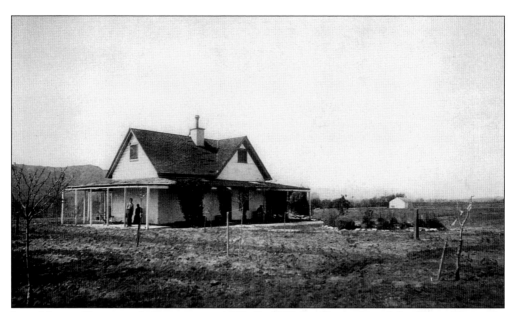

JOSE MARIA GONZALEZ'S RESIDENCE, 1879. In 1879, Jose built this adobe. He and his wife, Grace, raised their children Ormiston and Ysabel here. Jose was considered one of Temecula's most prominent citizens. He was the deputy assessor in 1884 when this area was San Diego County, before the formation of Riverside County in 1893. He was Riverside County's first tax collector and was a trustee of the Temecula School. (Courtesy of Barnett collection.)

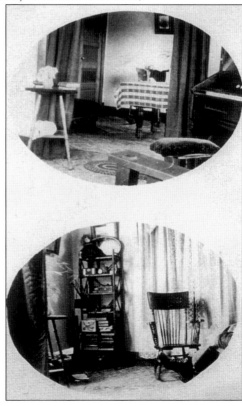

INSIDE GONZALEZ ADOBE. Adobe bricks made of clay, straw, and water were the most common building material in the Temecula region in times past. This picture postcard shows the comfortable interior of the Gonzalez adobe, which is still standing. The card, sent by Ormiston's wife, Maude, to her mother, Mrs. C. A. Van Nest, in Los Angeles, reads, "Dearest Mama, We got home all O.K. Have been working in the yard this morning. Write when you can. Much love, Maude." (Courtesy of Barnett collection.)

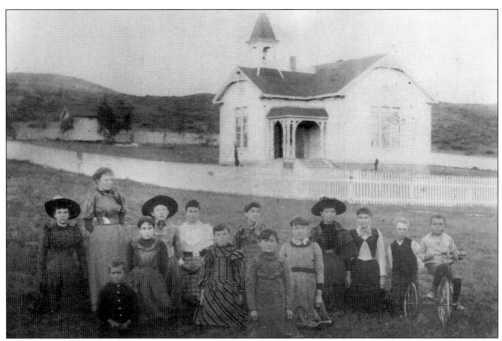

PUJOL SCHOOL AND STUDENTS. This early photograph shows students at the Pujol School, which was located where the Temecula Valley Museum is today. Pujol School was named for Mercedes Pujol, who stayed with the Gonzalez' when she came from Spain to settle her late husband's estate. She donated land for the school and for a public cemetery. The small structure at the back left is an outhouse. Ysabel Gonzalez is the sixth person from the left, wearing the white lacy blouse. (Courtesy of Barnett collection.)

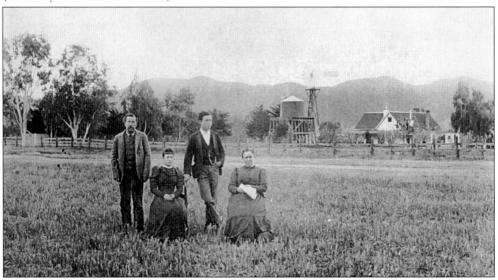

JOSE GONZALEZ AND FAMILY, 1894. Jose, with his daughter Ysabel "Bessie," son Ormiston "Ormie," and wife, Grace, sitting, pose in the field south of the family home. Grace came to California as a governess for the Sumner family in Elsinore. Jose met Grace while helping Mr. Sumner build a fireplace that did not pour smoke into his house. Love bloomed. All of Jose's family is buried in the Temecula Public Cemetery. (Courtesy of Barnett collection.)

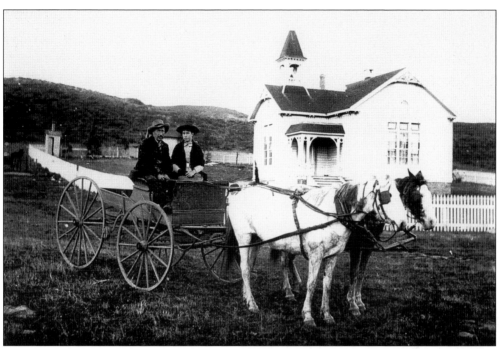

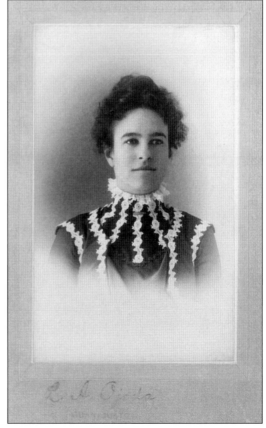

JOSE GONZALEZ AND DAUGHTER YSABEL.
Jose encouraged education. Ysabel
completed her primary education at the
Pujol School in the background. Since
there was not a secondary school nearby,
she went to Mexico to stay with relatives
while she completed her education in
the Spanish tradition. She married
Adrian B. "Ben" Barnett. The Temecula
School Board named Ysabel Barnett
Elementary School in her honor.
(Courtesy of Barnett collection.)

YSABEL "BESSIE" GONZALEZ, 1879–1969.
Ysabel was the first non-Indian girl born
and raised in Temecula. Her father was
from Spain and her mother was from
England. This photograph was taken
while she was in high school in Mexico.
She wrote on the photograph, *"Para Papa
y Mamma de Bessie, 30 Octubre 1901."*
(Courtesy of Barnett collection.)

51

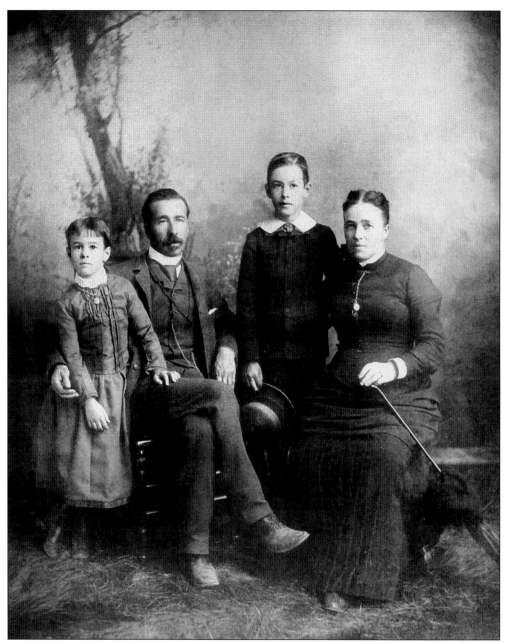

GONZALEZ FAMILY PORTRAIT. Jose Maria Gonzalez (1835–1921), Grace Street Gonzalez (1846–1933), Ormiston Gonzalez (1877–1954), and Ysabel Gonzalez (1879–1969) sit for a family portrait in the 1880s. Ormiston was named after Jose's first wife, Margaret Ormiston, who died at sea on their way from Scotland to California. (Courtesy of Barnett collection.)

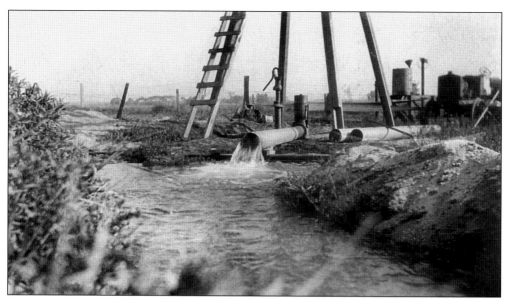

GONZALEZ WELL. When a well was dug and water accessed, the family celebrated. Without water, farming operations could not survive. The Gonzalez' well provided water for the household and for their alfalfa fields and fruit trees. (Courtesy of Barnett collection.)

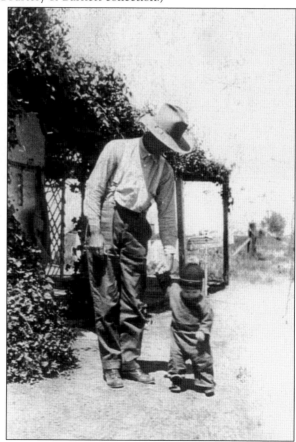

ORMISTON "ORMIE" AND SON FRANK. In 1919, Ormie's son Frank became the first and only baby born in the Gonzalez adobe. Frank moved to Escondido, where he was a tile setter and a talented oil painter. (Courtesy of Barnett collection.)

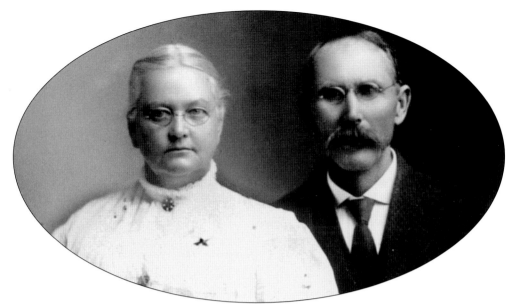

ELI AND ALICE BARNETT, 1917. Eli Elsa Barnett was born in Illinois in 1852 and came to California with his father in 1869, going first to the Northern California gold fields before becoming one of Temecula's leading ranchers and stockmen. In 1875, he married Alice. This photograph was taken in 1917 when they took a trip to Oklahoma to visit relatives. (Courtesy of June Roripaugh Tull.)

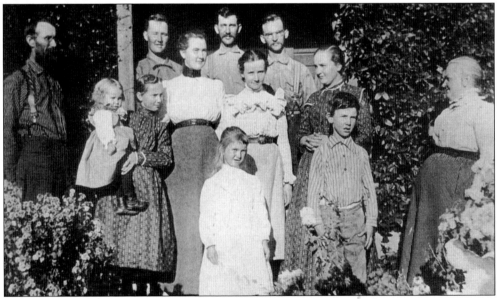

ELI AND ALICE BARNETT'S FAMILY, EARLY 1900S. Pictured here are (first row) Ruth, who married Charles McClintock, a worker at the Alberhill brick factory; Anson Alden, who married Jessie Smith; and mother Alice; (second row) Eli and Alice's unidentified grandchild; Lena; Myrtle, who married Ray Roripaugh; Pearl, who married Jack Roripaugh; Sarah, who, with her husband, Charles Clogston, started Mothers Cafe, now known as Swing Inn; and (third row) father Eli; Cephas Logan, who operated a store on Main Street; Mark, a farmer; and Adrian "Ben," who married Ysabel Gonzalez.

This is a page from a promotional booklet, "Tempting Thriving, Temecula," published c. 1901–1910. The photograph below was featured with the article.

E. E. BARNETT

Two and a half miles north of the town of Temecula is situated a splendid ranch property which well illustrates the fertility of valley soil when intelligently tilled and farmed. Reference is had to the 1200 acre farm of E. E. Barnett, which is a portion of the old historic Murrieta ranch and which was purchased of the original owner by Mr. Barnett eight years ago.

The Barnett ranch is primarily devoted to the raising of barley and wheat, fine horses, thoroughbred and standard, and thoroughbred Hereford bulls; but pears, prunes, plums, apples, apricots and other fruits are raised for family consumption and all bear prolifically. Mr. Barnett's income last year from the sale of horses alone was $5000.00 and his revenue from the various products of the ranch is a princely one.

E. E. Barnett is a native of Illinois, but is a California pioneer and was one of the earliest ranchers of the famed Big Semi Valley in Ventura.

He and his winsome helpmeet, who was Miss Alice A. Stevens, an Iowa girl, have raised a large family of boys and girls who are now prominent in the valley's business and social life.

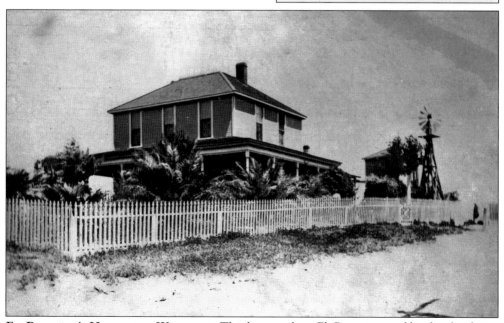

ELI BARNETT'S HOUSE AND WINDMILL. This house, where Eli Barnett raised his family of nine children, sat on Jefferson Avenue near Santa Gertrudis Creek. His daughter Ruth was married in this house and his grandson Leo Roripaugh was born there. In 1941, Henry Boohtger dismantled the house. (Courtesy of June Roripaugh Tull.)

ADRIAN BENJAMIN "BEN" BARNETT, 1879–1950. In 1905, Ben, Eli and Alice's third son, married Ysabel "Bessie" Gonzalez. He farmed alfalfa and operated a dairy ranch on 200 acres two miles north of Old Town Temecula. He ran 60 head of cattle and shipped about 10 gallons of cream daily to the Arlington Creamery near Riverside. He served as a judge from 1940 to 1950, was a member of the Elsinore Masonic Lodge, served as president of the Elsinore High School Board, and worked at Guenther's Murrieta Hot Springs Resort as a purchasing agent. (Courtesy of Barnett collection.)

YSABEL "BESSIE" AND RALPH BARNETT. This is Ysabel with her first son, Ralph. In later years, her three boys formed a band with Max Thompson and other locals. They played for dances at schools and churches from Mount Palomar to Elsinore, significant distances to travel in the 1920s. For Ysabel, those were some of her happiest memories, as her three boys were her pride and joy. She was also a past matron of the Elsinore Eastern Star. This photograph was taken by F. L. Fernald, an early Temecula photographer. (Courtesy of Barnett collection.)

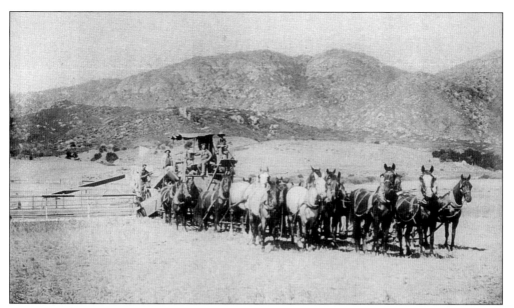

BEN BARNETT WITH HORSES, 1900. Pulling a harvester, Ben Barnett drives a team of about 20 horses. The driver of the combined header and harvester was called a mule skinner. He sat high above the team holding the jerk line to the lead animals. When mechanized tractors and Caterpillar machinery replaced animals, the drivers became known as cat skinners. (Courtesy of Barnett collection.)

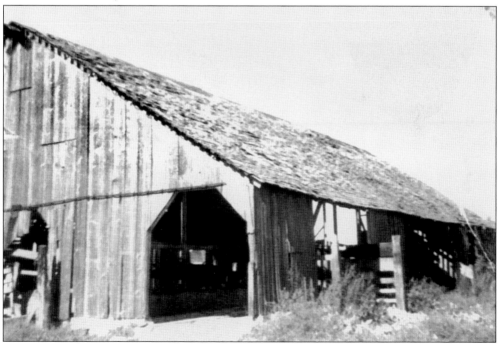

BEN BARNETT'S BARN. The Barnett dairy barn is in full swing. The cows were milked by hand here before milking machines were invented. Stanchions, or braces, located along the feed troughs, held the cows in place for milking. The barn was also used for hay storage. (Courtesy of Barnett collection.)

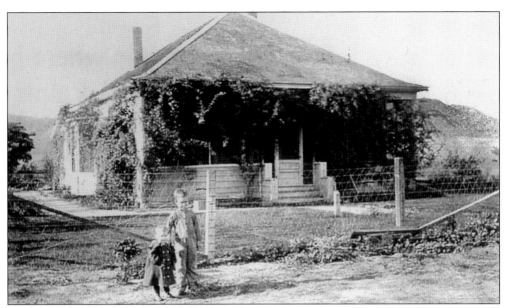

BEN BARNETT'S HOUSE, 1914. Ralph Barnett, the oldest of Ben and Ysabel's children, plays with his sister Adrienne Grace, who died in 1918 at the age of five. Ralph and his brothers Chester and Francis were encouraged to bring friends from town to their ranch home. They became pals with Horace Parker, the only child of the depot agent. Parker spent his later years writing the history of Temecula, an avocation inspired by stories he heard "Aunt Bessie" tell when he visited this house. (Courtesy of Barnett collection.)

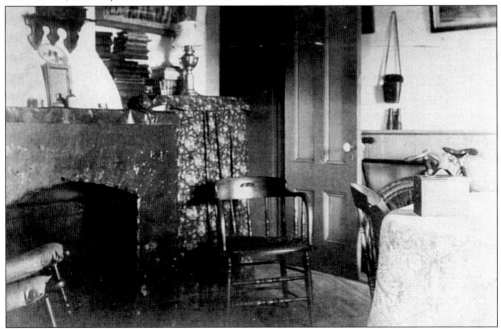

INSIDE BEN BARNETT'S HOME. This photograph (from a postcard) shows the room where Judge Ben Barnett held court. The captain's chairs are now in Malcolm and Loretta Barnett's home and some of the other furniture is in the Historic Temecula Hotel owned by the Horace and Leverne Parker estate. (Courtesy of Barnett collection.)

MALCOLM BARNETT'S BLOCKS BY JUDGE BARNETT'S DESK. This is the old roll-top desk Judge Barnett used for holding court in the dining room of the old ranch house. The desk is presently in the old Temecula Hotel owned by the estate of Horace and Leverne Parker. (Courtesy of Barnett collection.)

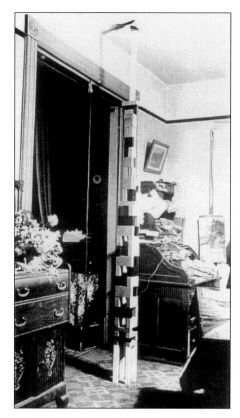

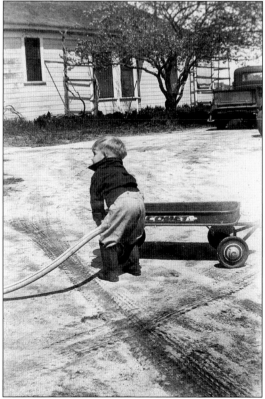

MALCOLM AND WAGON OUTSIDE BARNETT HOME. Malcolm Barnett, a great-grandson of both Jose Gonzalez and E. E. Barnett, is pretending to fill his wagon with gasoline at the ranch of his grandparents, Mr. and Mrs. Ben Barnett. Malcolm, Ralph Barnett's son, graduated from Temecula Grammar School and Elsinore High School. Now a retired firefighter from the San Diego Fire Department, he is a volunteer docent at the Temecula Valley Museum. He enjoys speaking to groups and giving tours of Old Town Temecula. He is active in several groups, including the Old Town Temecula Gunfighters. (Courtesy of Barnett collection.)

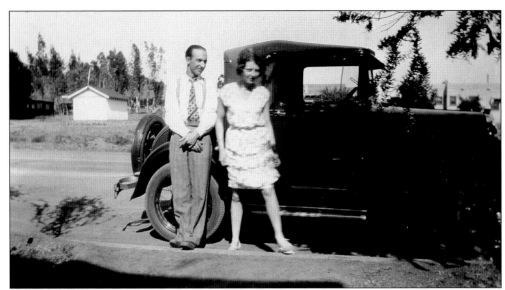

RALPH AND MARY BARNETT. This is a photograph of Ralph Barnett, the first son of Ben and Ysabel Barnett, and his Elsinore High School sweetheart Mary, shortly after they were married. When Ralph was a young man, he played the saxophone in a band with his mother and brothers. Ralph, Eli Barnett's grandson, was an accountant for Guenther's Murrieta Hot Springs Resort. After he retired, they moved to Hemet. (Courtesy of Barnett collection.)

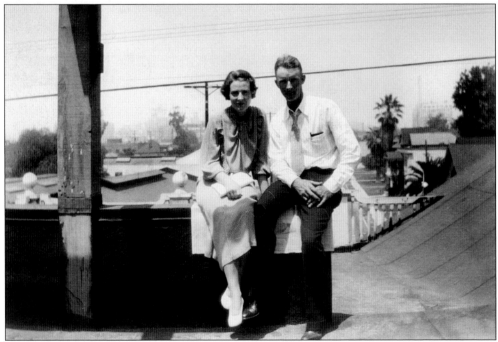

MARIAN AND LEO RORIPAUGH. Leo, Eli Barnett's grandson, married his high school sweetheart Marian Elliot from Elsinore. Leo became a successful rancher and farmer. The Roripaugh Hills development is named for this rancher and his family. Marian took business courses at Redlands College before they were married. She played the violin and was a talented painter. (Courtesy of June Roripaugh Tull.)

LEO RORIPAUGH, AGE FIVE. Leo, his brother Louis "Louie," and their sister Margaret lived in the caretaker's house on the Pauba Ranch while their father Jack was foreman. After graduation from Temecula Grammar School and Elsinore High School, Leo did bookkeeping for the Vails and took many of Mahlon Vail's friends on hunting trips. In 1948, he started farming 80 acres on Winchester Road between Interstate 15 and Margarita Road. (Courtesy of June Roripaugh Tull.)

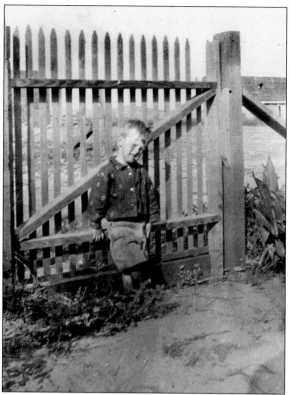

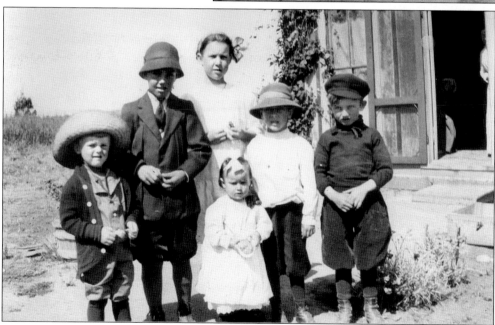

ELI BARNETT'S GRANDCHILDREN IN FALLBROOK, 1915. Eli and Alice Barnett's grandchildren pose at a home on Gird Road in Fallbrook. Pictured here, from left to right, are (first row) Margaret Roripaugh; (second row) Leo Roripaugh, Barney Roripaugh, Eldred Roripaugh, Ralph Barnett, and Louie Roripaugh. (Courtesy of June Roripaugh Tull.)

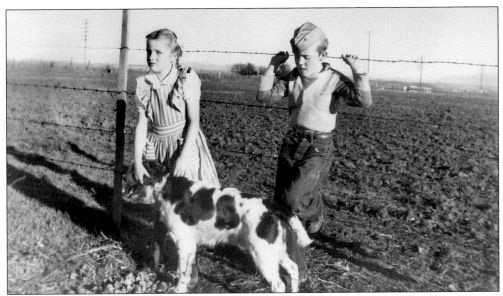

JACK AND JUNE RORIPAUGH WITH SARGE. June and Jack Roripaugh, children of Leo and Marian, pose with their dog at the family home just north of the corner of present-day Winchester Road and Jefferson Avenue. Jack and June each graduated from Temecula Grammar School and Elsinore High School, where June was a cheerleader. Jack married and raised his family in Temecula. He operates heavy equipment and does work for the developer who is building residential homes on some of the former Roripaugh property. June married and raised her family in Palmer, Alaska. The Roripaughs have always been hard workers and lovers of the land. (Courtesy of June Roripaugh Tull.)

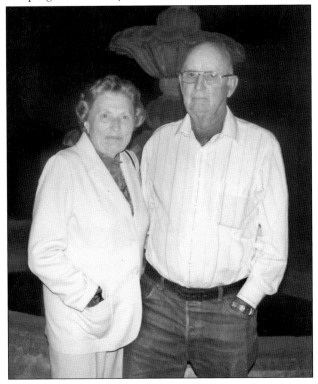

MARIAN AND LEO RORIPAUGH IN THEIR GOLDEN YEARS. This couple watched the Temecula Valley change from open space with ranches and houses that were miles apart to densely packed housing tracts. They seldom saw cars on the dirt roads throughout the countryside that have now grown to the six and eight lanes of pavement filled with cars. (Courtesy of June Roripaugh Tull.)

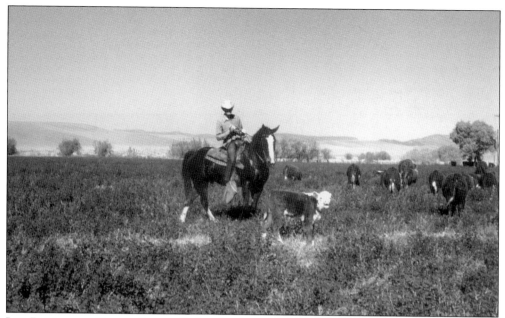

LEO RORIPAUGH RIDING FLASH. Riding his favorite horse, Leo oversees some of his cattle. The Roripaugh cows birthed about 100 calves each spring. The animals were branded and vaccinated for Black Leg disease, then put out to pasture. When the cattle were about 18 months old, they were shipped to a feedlot in Walnut, California, where they were fattened to 1,000 or 1,200 pounds. They were then sold to the Cudahy Packing Plant. (Courtesy of June Roripaugh Tull.)

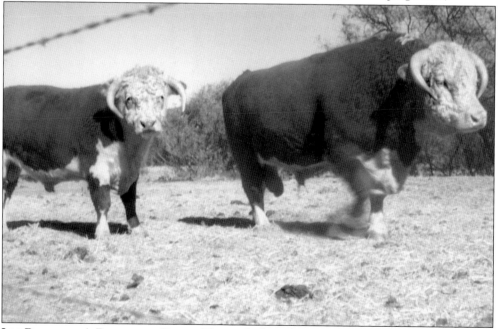

LEO RORIPAUGH'S REGISTERED BULLS. The two bulls in the photograph were registered Herefords. During the 1940s and 1950s, registered bulls cost an average of $3,500 to $4,000 each. Leo kept one bull for each 50 cows. The bulls were bred with average cattle to produce prime beef. (Courtesy of June Roripaugh Tull.)

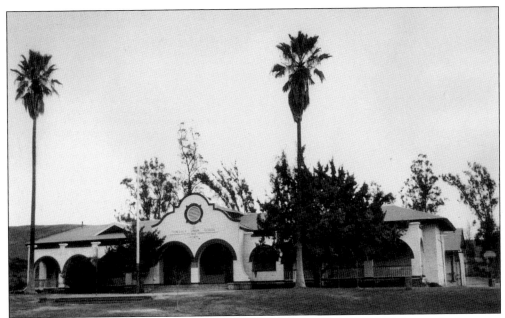

TEMECULA UNION SCHOOL. This building was built in 1915 for $10,000. Located where the Temecula Valley Museum is now, it housed two classrooms, an office, and a 20-foot by 30-foot auditorium. Around 1938, an older school was moved from Pala Road to provide an additional classroom. In 1971, the school pictured here burned down. (Courtesy of Knott family.)

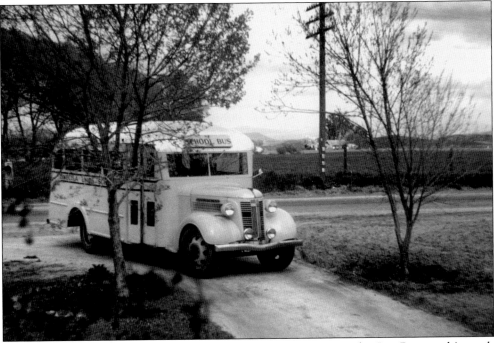

TEMECULA SCHOOL BUS. The Temecula school bus is turning around at Leo Roripaugh's ranch on Highway 395, now Jefferson Avenue. The bus picked up students who lived on the outskirts of town. Vernon and Annie Knott and Vern Otto drove the bus for many years. (Courtesy of June Roripaugh Tull.)

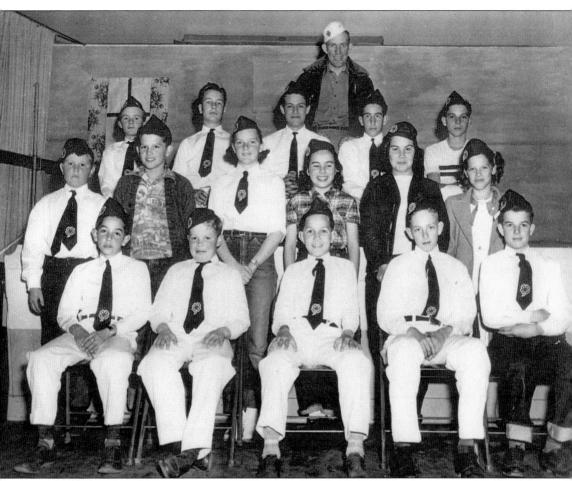

TEMECULA 4-H CLUB. Pictured, from left to right, these members of the 1949 Temecula 4-H Club are (first row) David Barnett, Andy McElhinney, Bobbie Barnett, Leon Borel, and Jim Ramsay; (second row) Fred Guenther, Charles Knott, June Roripaugh, Louise Roripaugh, Ann Wagner, and Vernett Knott; (third row) Jack Roripaugh, Dick Barnett, Alex Borel, Malcolm Barnett, and Lyn Thomas. Dick Ramsay, their leader standing at the top, was a border patrol agent. Eight of the 16 club members were great-grandchildren of Eli Barnett. Every year, each child raised a calf purchased from the Vail Ranch. They showed their livestock at the Hemet Farmers Fair and sold them to the highest bidder. Local restaurateurs would pay higher than normal prices for the beef to support the 4-H program. (Courtesy of Barnett collection.)

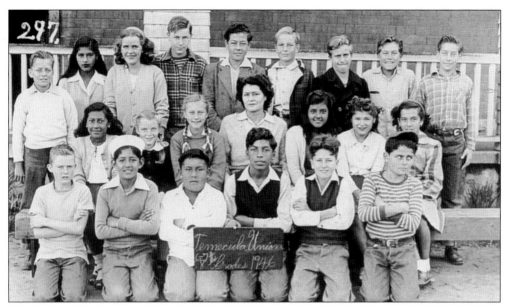

CLASS OF 1946. Students of the sixth, seventh, and eighth grades pose with their teacher Nida Ashman, who was raised in the Temecula Valley. Nida's father, Tony Ashman, a Pechanga Indian, lived to be 101 years old. He remembered seeing Louis and Ramona Wolf, and he recalled stories told by his parents about the eviction of the Temecula Indians. (Courtesy of Barnett collection.)

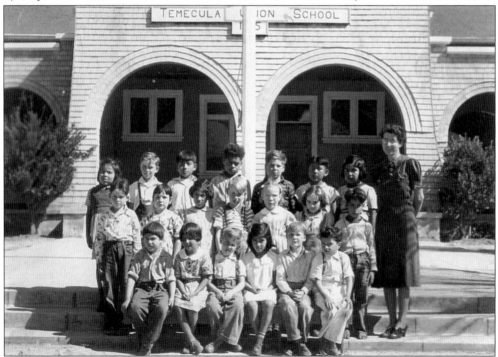

FIRST AND SECOND GRADES, TEMECULA GRAMMAR SCHOOL, 1939–1940. These students were taught in one room. They were not required to wear shoes to attend. Several of the students pictured here still live in the Temecula Valley. Some were from the Pechanga Reservation. (Courtesy of Barnett collection.)

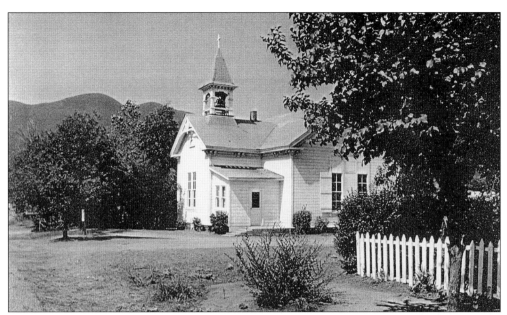

"Mrs. Knott's Church." Freda Knott taught Sunday school in this building when it was located on Fourth Street in Old Town Temecula. It was originally the Pujol schoolhouse located where the Temecula Valley Museum is today. Each Thursday, during the 1940s and 1950s, the Roman Catholic students at the public school would go to St. Catherine's Church for catechism. Mrs. Knott provided religious education for the Protestant students at the same time as the catechism classes. The building is now open for public tours at 29825 Santiago Road. (Courtesy of Knott family.)

St. Catherine of Alexandria Catholic Church. This was the first church built in Temecula. Constructed in 1917, the 26-foot by 36-foot building cost $1,200. To help pay for the building, Mahlon Vail hosted a fund-raiser. He donated a steer for the barbecue and dance party at Pauba Ranch. The building, originally stained a dark brown color, was later painted white. The building has been moved to Sam Hicks Monument, where it is used as a wedding chapel. The growing congregation now meets in a modern building a short distance from "Mrs. Knott's Church" on Santiago Road. (Courtesy of Knott family.)

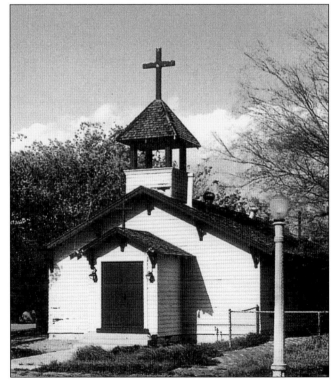

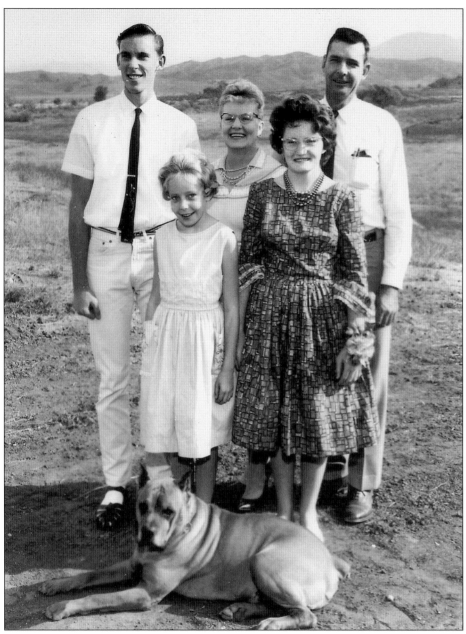

SAM HICKS AND FAMILY. Sam Hicks Jr., Nancy, Ruby, Susan, and Sam pose with their dog. Sam met the famous Temecula author Erle Stanley Gardner when Sam guided one of "Uncle Erle's" expeditions through the Wyoming backcountry. Erle invited Sam to manage his Rancho Paisano near Temecula and Sam spent the rest of his life in Temecula, except for when he was traveling with Uncle Erle. Sam became an author and photographer of note and was one of the founders of the *High Country* magazine. He was responsible for the "They Passed this Way" monument honoring pioneers who came through Temecula during the early years. Sam was also a constable. After suffering the tragic loss of his wife, Ruby, daughter Susan, and the dog in a tragic car accident, his son was killed in the line of duty as a peace officer. His surviving child Nancy grew up in Temecula, and her daughter Theresa teaches in Murrieta. (Courtesy of June Roripaugh Tull.)

Five

AERIAL VIEWS

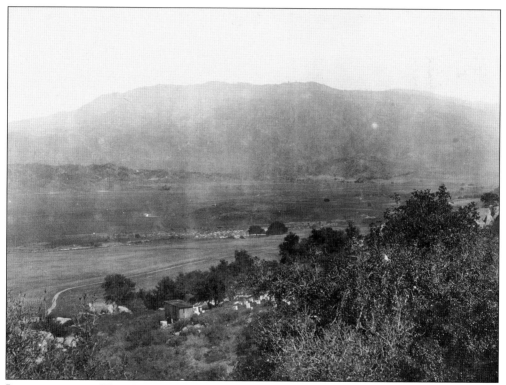

LOOKING ACROSS WOLF VALLEY TOWARD PALOMAR MOUNTAIN. Awaiting transportation out of the valley in about 1914, slabs of granite rest on a hillside near the Rainbow Grade overlooking the Wolf Valley. The building in the foreground was a storage shed for explosives used in the nearby granite quarry. The foundation was still visible in 2004, and an old-timer told about finding remnants of explosives inside the shed in the 1950s. Looking toward the mountain from the shed, the bright white spot was the schoolhouse located at what is now the northwest corner of Pechanga Parkway and Loma Linda Road. To the right of the schoolhouse is the column of the Wolf Monument. The photograph was probably taken by F. L. Fernald, a local photographer who also owned a quarry and an automobile garage. He shaped his granite into cemetery headstones. (Courtesy of the Seay family.)

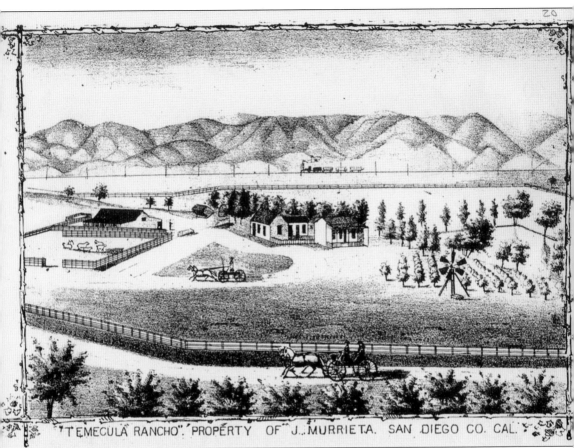

"TEMECULA RANCHO". PROPERTY OF J. MURRIETA. SAN DIEGO CO. CAL.

SKETCH OF JUAN MURRIETA'S RANCHO. Juan Murrieta's property was on what is now known as Jefferson Avenue, near Winchester Road. Murrieta, a Spaniard, arrived in the Temecula area about 1870, already a successful sheep rancher and businessman with a herd of 100,000 sheep. He purchased Ranchos Temecula and Pauba. He was in the posse led by the San Diego County sheriff that evicted the Temecula Indians from their ancestral home. This sketch was made sometime after the train came to the valley in 1882. (Courtesy of Jack Roripaugh.)

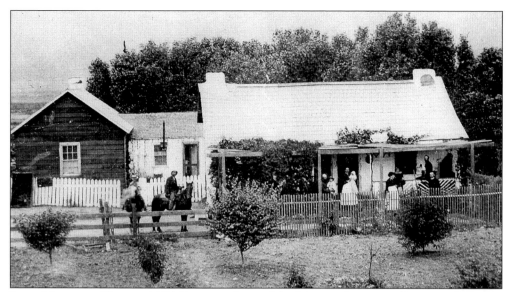

JUAN MURRIETA HOUSE, 1887. Posing in front of the Murrieta house are Ormiston Gonzalez, Ami Golsh, Juan Murrieta, his son Henry, Mrs. Murrieta, her daughter Lita, Mrs. Worthington, her daughter Henrietta, Mr. Butcher, and a Catholic priest. Juan Murrieta retained this home acreage after he and his brother Ezequiel sold all but 1,000 acres to the Temecula Land and Water Company in 1884. The town of Murrieta was named in his honor. (Courtesy of Horace and Leverne Parker Collection.)

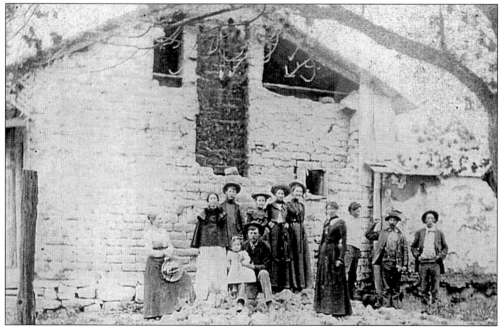

MURRIETA'S HOUSE AFTER 1899 EARTHQUAKE. People stand by the north wall of the Murrieta adobe after it sustained irreparable damage during the 1899 earthquake that struck on Christmas Day. Some of the foundation of this adobe, where Ysabel "Bessie" Gonzalez was born, remained after Leo Roripaugh built his ranch home in front of it. (Courtesy of Horace and Leverne Parker Collection.)

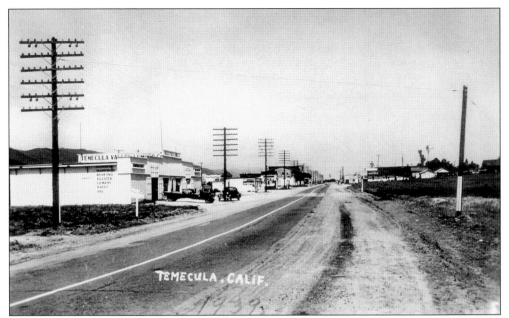

HIGHWAY 395, LOOKING NORTH, 1939. This rare photograph shows the main business district of Temecula along the highway, now known as Old Town Front Street. The lumber company on the left was where The Stampede is today. Farther down the left side of the street is the two-story Welty Building. (Courtesy of Barnett collection.)

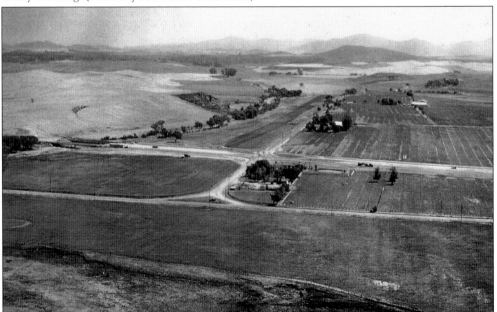

AERIAL VIEW OF WINCHESTER ROAD, 1950s. Looking east along Winchester Road from Highway 395, now called Jefferson Avenue, only farmland is seen. The home in the center belonged to Dick and Margaret Ramsay. Dick was a border patrol agent and a 4-H leader. Margaret, the daughter of Jack Roripaugh Sr., owned an antique shop. Her parents lived in the house just to the east. After Winchester Road was paved, between 1927 and 1930, it was called State Highway 79. (Courtesy of Jack Roripaugh.)

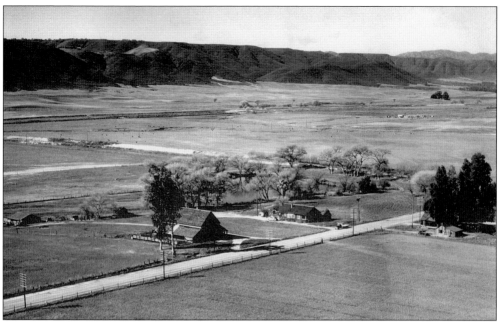

LEO RORIPAUGH'S HOME AND BARN ON OLD HIGHWAY 395. Looking northwest, this view shows the Leo Roripaugh home during the mid-1940s at the site of the earlier Juan Murrieta adobe. The water in the reservoir between the trees west of the house irrigated fields before flowing into the Murrieta Creek. (Courtesy of Jack Roripaugh.)

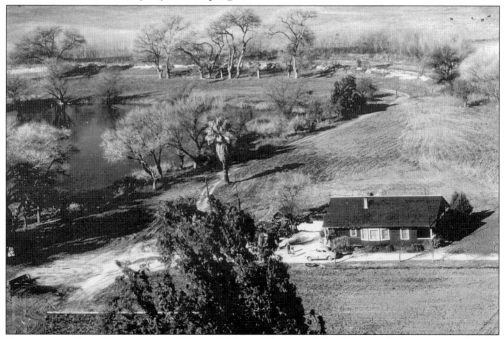

CLOSEUP OF LEO RORIPAUGH'S HOME. This aerial view of the Roripaugh home was taken in January 1945. The Juan Murrieta adobe stood just to the left of the large tree in the foreground. One of the pear trees Murrieta planted still bore fruit at the time the photograph was taken. (Courtesy of Jack Roripaugh.)

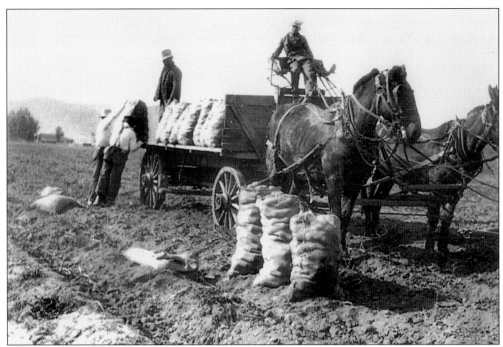

POTATO FIELD, 1917. This field was where the Sears Store of Temecula's Promenade Mall is today. Jack and Pearl Roripaugh's home in the background was on Winchester Road, east of Ynez. Eli Barnett's oldest son Mark is at the back of the wagon, and Mark's son Richard, age nine, is on the seat driving the team of horses. Richard was one of the children sitting on the wagon on the opening page of Chapter 4. (Courtesy of Barnett collection.)

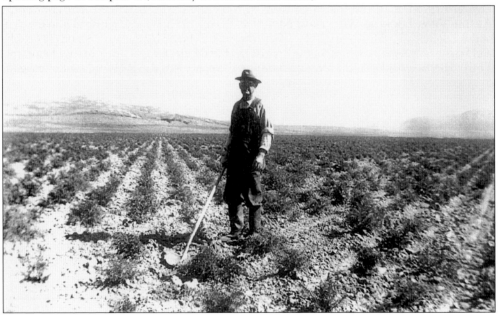

MARK BARNETT, 1940S. This view from Winchester Road looks south to Mark Barnett's fields where the Promenade Mall is today. The crop may be sugar beets, or it may be carrots grown for their seeds. (Courtesy of Barnett collection.)

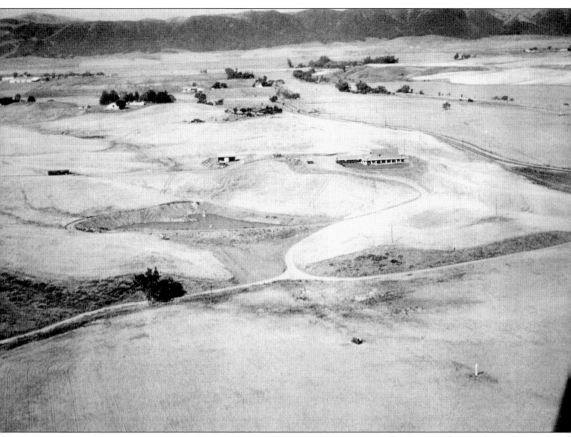

AERIAL VIEW, LOOKING WEST FROM NICHOLAS ROAD, 1975. Winchester Road is to the right of the first house in the picture. Today Chaparral High School is at the intersection of Nicholas and Winchester Roads. Grading for the Roripaugh Hills development is visible in the photograph. The Promenade Mall is in the location shown in the upper left. (Courtesy of Jack Roripaugh.)

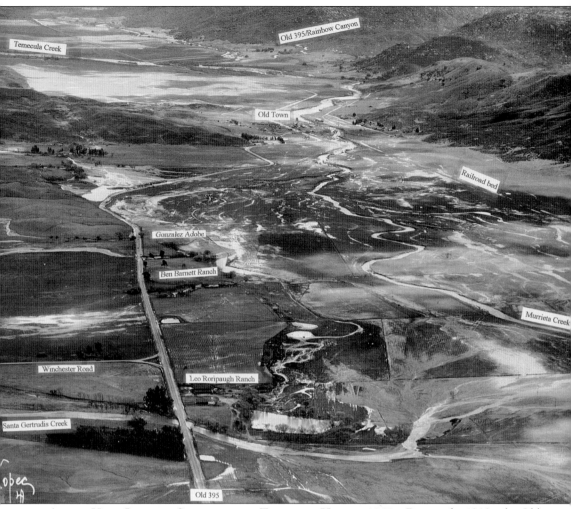

Temecula Creek

Old 395/Rainbow Canyon

Old Town

Railroad bed

Gonzalez Adobe

Ben Barnett Ranch

Murrieta Creek

Winchester Road

Leo Roripaugh Ranch

Santa Gertrudis Creek

Old 395

AERIAL VIEW, LOOKING SOUTH ACROSS TEMECULA VALLEY, 1940S. During the 1940s, the Old Highway 395 wound from Riverside to Perris, Elsinore, Murrieta, Temecula, and through Rainbow Canyon to Fallbrook. The valley was sparsely populated and had ample water. The railroad bed is near the foothills of the mountains and the Murrieta and Santa Gertrudis Creeks are shown in this photograph. The Temecula Valley Museum now sits north of Old Town where the cluster of trees is. In 1949, Highway 395 bypassed Temecula with a divided highway. (Courtesy of Jack Roripaugh.)

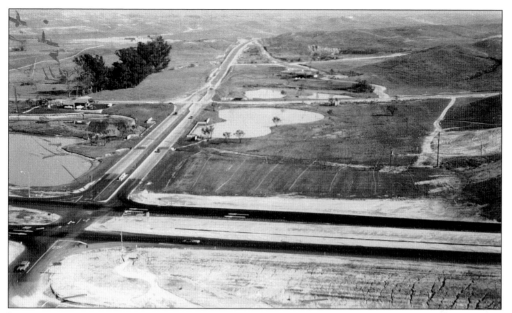

Looking East from Intersection of Highway 395 and Rancho California Road, 1969. The pond on the left is still in the Tower Plaza shopping center, originally called the Rancho California Plaza. Marie Callender's Restaurant sits at the location of the pond in the lower right, and the duck pond is still at the corner of Ynez and Rancho California Roads. (Courtesy of Jack Roripaugh.)

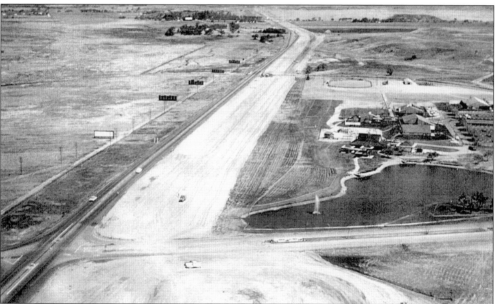

Looking North along Construction of Interstate 15, 1975. In 1964, when the Vail Ranch was sold to Kaiser Aetna, a planned community was laid out and things began to change. This shows the construction of the interstate highway near Rancho California Road with the first modern shopping center at the right. Above "The Plaza," as the shopping center was called, is an arena for a rodeo. The vacant land on the left side was designated for an industrial park. (Courtesy of Jack Roripaugh.)

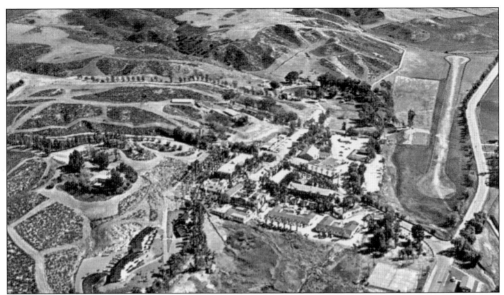

AERIAL VIEW OF GUENTHER'S MURRIETA HOT SPRINGS RESORT. Fritz Guenther purchased the Murrieta Hot Springs from a Pasadena woman in 1902 and developed it into a tourist destination. Early guests arrived by automobile or bus to enjoy mud baths and hot mineral water. Sports activities included croquet, horseshoes, miniature golf, swimming, and tennis. In later years, dancing, golf, horseback riding, and motion pictures were added for guest enjoyment. At right is Murrieta Hot Springs Road. This is the front of a business card for the resort. (Courtesy of Guenther family.)

Guenther's Murrieta Hot Springs

Nestled on the sun-drenched slopes of Riverside County in Southern California is Guenther's Murrieta Hot Springs Resort, a world-famous spa which, for several generations, has brought health, happiness and rejuvenation to thousands of people. The healing properties of its waters, outstanding accommodations and food, superb baths and treatments, the facilities for sports and recreation, and the moderation of its prices—all these factors have combined to make Guenther's Murrieta Hot Springs Southern California's best liked resort. At an elevation of 1309 ft., it has a near-perfect climate.

AREA CODE 714

MURRIETA, CALIFORNIA 92362

677-2311

FRED GUENTHER-MGR.

TEXT ON REVERSE OF GUENTHER'S MURRIETA HOT SPRINGS RESORT BUSINESS CARD. This business card was first used by Fritz Guenther's son Fred when he took over management of the resort. Native Americans first noticed the springs' healing properties. The site was later developed as a place where Hollywood celebrities and businessmen and their families would come to spend several weeks of vacation. It is now the setting of a Bible college and Christian retreat center. (Courtesy of Guenther family.)

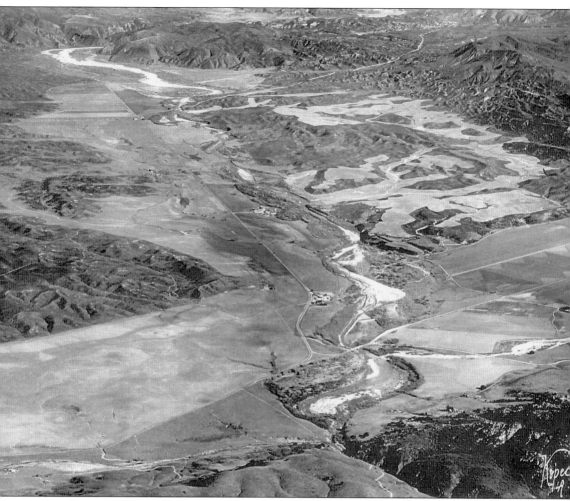

AERIAL VIEW OF WOLF VALLEY, LOOKING EAST. Highway 79 South is in the center of the picture heading toward Aguanga. The Temecula Creek meanders approximately parallel to the road. The McSweeneys leased buildings, seen just below the center of the photograph, from the Vails. The group of buildings in the center is the Vail Ranch headquarters, which was developed around the historic Wolf Store. (Courtesy of Jack Roripaugh.)

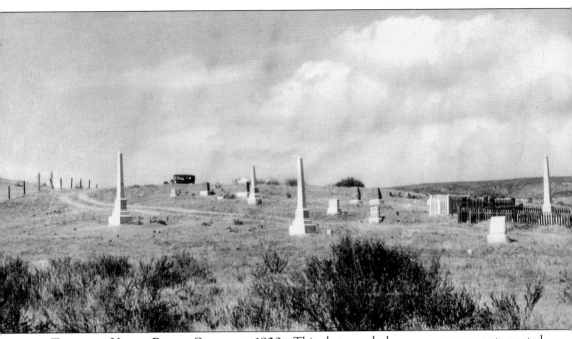

Temecula Valley Public Cemetery, 1920s. This photograph shows some monuments erected in memory of early area residents in the graveyard at the end of C Street near Santiago Road. Most of the granite for the monuments was quarried south of Temecula. The land for the cemetery was given by Mercedes Pujol, the widow of Domingo Pujol, when she came from Spain to Temecula in 1884 to settle her husband's estate. She specified the land she gave was for a public burial ground. She also donated the land for the Pujol School, where the Temecula Valley Museum is today. The oldest marker in the cemetery is dated 1894. (Courtesy of Barnett collection.)

Six

RANCHING IN PAUBA VALLEY

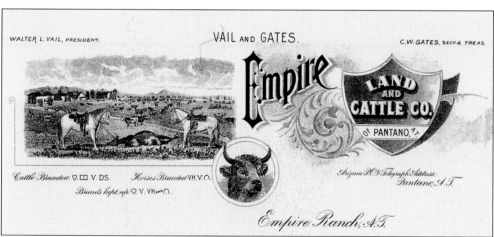

EMPIRE RANCH LETTERHEAD. This letterhead is from the Empire Ranch in Arizona that Walter Vail and partners developed into a huge cattle enterprise. The endeavor was successful enough to spread across five states. The Vails bought controlling water rights, and they each served on the Pima County Board of Supervisors. Walter served on the Arizona Territorial Legislature. From the ranch, Walter's brother Ed Vail and some of their cowboys drove 900 steers to pastureland near Warner Springs, California. (Courtesy of Sandy Wilkinson.)

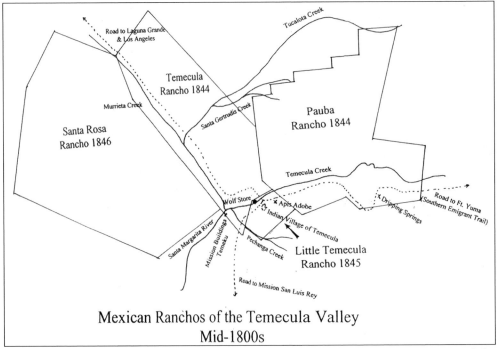

Mexican Ranchos of the Temecula Valley
Mid-1800s

MAP OF MEXICAN RANCHOS, MID-1800s. This diagram depicts the configuration of the Temecula area prior to the completion of the railroad that moved the center of activity from the region of the Wolf Store to present-day Old Town Temecula. Dripping Springs was a stop along the Butterfield Stage Route to water horses. The four Mexican ranchos were purchased in 1905 to form the 87,500-acre Vail Ranch. (Courtesy of VaRRA.)

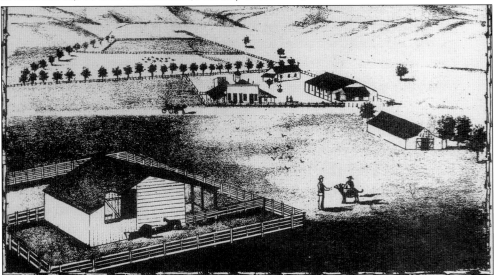

SKETCH OF THE WOLF RANCHO, 1883. Itinerant artists went through the country during this era, and for a fee, sketched ranchos for the owners. This sketch shows the Wolf Store, the Old Butterfield Stage Road, and the Wolf residence, which later became the Vail Ranch cookhouse. It also shows fenced fields, trees, and two barns. Behind the Wolf Store is a structure some think may have been the first school in the area. (Courtesy of Sandy Wilkinson.)

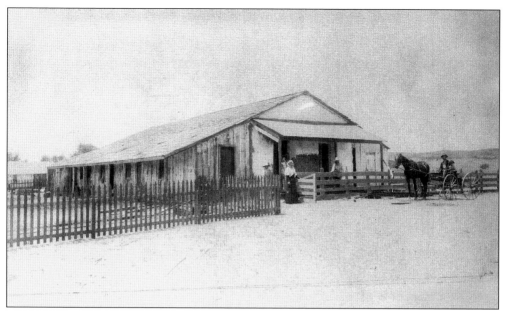

RAMONA WOLF OUTSIDE THE WOLF STORE, 1891. Ramona Wolf stands in front of the Wolf Store, the general merchandise market that she and her husband ran. Along the south side of the store were hotel rooms for travelers who came in stagecoaches and mud wagons. The road in the foreground is the Old Butterfield Stage Route. Fences were needed to keep horses and other animals from wandering too close to the front of the store. (Courtesy of Ramona Pageant Association.)

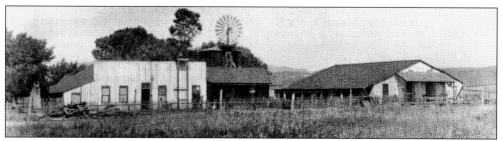

WOLF STORE AT THE LUDY RANCH, 1902. After Louis Wolf died in 1887, Jacob Ludy purchased the ranch. This picture shows an addition to the residence that later became the Vail Ranch cookhouse. Some think the addition was the schoolhouse building shown in the sketch on the previous page. (Courtesy of Horace and Leverne Parker Collection.)

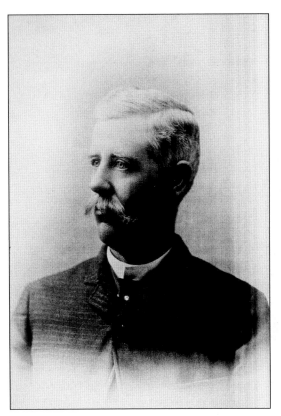

WALTER VAIL, 1852–1906. Walter Vail started the Vail Ranch, part of his five-state cattle empire. Born in Nova Scotia, Walter first came west to work in the silver mines in Nevada. After becoming disillusioned about life in a mining town, he started his cattle empire near Tucson, Arizona. Always looking for pastureland, he discovered the verdant valleys of Warner Ranch and Temecula. He favored Temecula because of the nearness to the railroad for transporting the cattle to market. (Courtesy of Sandy Wilkinson.)

MARGARET NEWHALL VAIL, 1854–1936. When Margaret Newhall married Walter Vail, he took her to the adobe house on the Empire Ranch that he improved from a primitive house with a dirt floor to a home suitable for a civilized woman. She raised their seven children in that house; it grew to 22 rooms with electricity and plumbing. The Vails were living in Los Angeles when Walter was fatally injured in a streetcar accident before the purchase of Temecula properties was completed. (Courtesy of Sandy Wilkinson.)

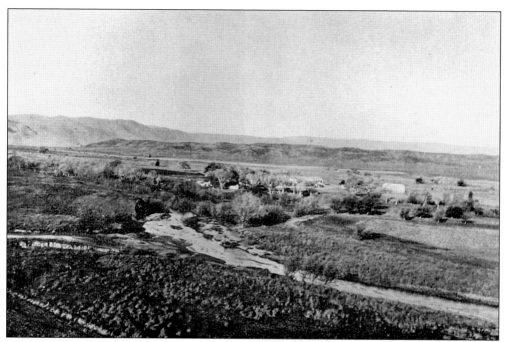

PANORAMA OF VAIL RANCH HEADQUARTERS SITE. This is a 1918 view of the Vail Ranch headquarters site from south of the Temecula Creek. It shows the river crossing where the Butterfield Stage and other conveyances crossed the creek, one of only a few such crossings because of the prevalence of quicksand in low creek areas. The abundance of water, vegetation, and game first made this site attractive to the Temecula Indians. The road later made it an important location for the townsite of Temecula around the Wolf Store. (Courtesy of 1919 Department of the Interior publication *Ground Water in the San Jacinto and Temecula Basins, California*.)

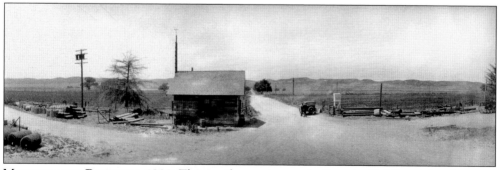

METEOROLOGY BUILDING, 1929. This weather station was built at the Vail Ranch headquarters because of a lawsuit in the 1910s about water rights. The suit was not settled until the mid-1940s. Data about rainfall, wind, and temperatures was collected here. In 1965, it became the first office for the Rancho California Water District. This photograph, taken by Ford A. Carpenter, shows Prof. G. A. Studensky from Moscow talking with F. A. Lyon at the rear of the automobile. (Courtesy of Sandy Wilkinson.)

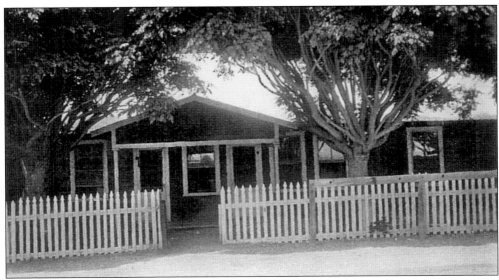

VAIL RANCH COOKHOUSE, 1928. The kitchen, a large pantry, and two walk-in refrigerator units were in this building. There were two dining rooms, one for the cowboys and ranch hands and the other for the VIPs like Mahlon Vail, Louie Roripaugh, and important visitors to the ranch. There were also bedrooms for the cook's family and the bookkeeper. (Courtesy of Edward G. Polley.)

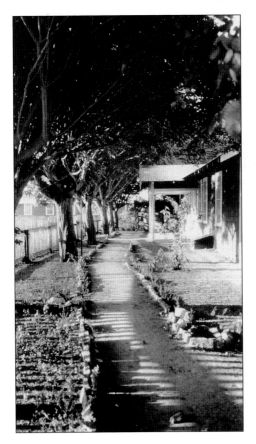

PATH IN FRONT OF COOKHOUSE. The pleasant walkway in front of the cookhouse looked like this during the Vail Ranch era. Ranch hands did not enter through the front door; instead, they would wash up at sinks outside and would enter a back door to the dining room. The picket fence was first erected when the Wolfs owned the property. Only a couple of the trees are still standing. A portion of the bunkhouse is visible through the trees on the left. (Courtesy of Sandy Wilkinson.)

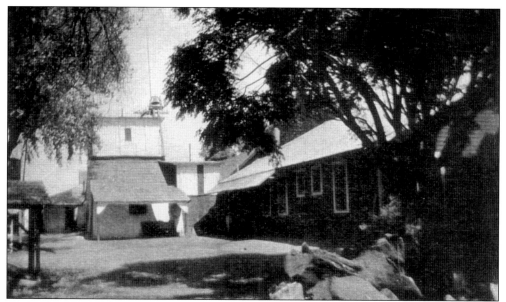

BACKSIDE OF COOKHOUSE. The white two-story building in the background is the water tank. A windmill pumps groundwater up to the tank. The water was stored up high so that the force of gravity creates water pressure when it goes through pipes and faucets in the house. The room under the water tank was cool and dairy products and other foodstuffs were kept cool there before electricity and refrigeration. The dinner bell called ranch workers to each meal and, in cases of emergencies, it called them to attention. The Vail Ranch was known for serving bountiful and good meals with steak, potatoes, and pitchers full of cold milk. (Courtesy of Edward G. Polley.)

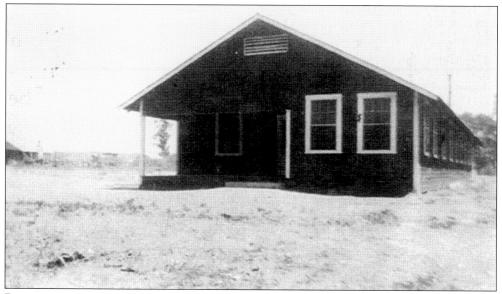

BUNKHOUSE AT VAIL RANCH. The bunkhouse had 12 two-man bedrooms, a sitting room with a central woodstove at the west end, and a bathroom and laundry room at the east end. The younger cowboys and ranch hands stayed here, but some of the older cowboys preferred living in the bunkrooms along the south side of the Wolf Store. (Courtesy of Edward G. Polley.)

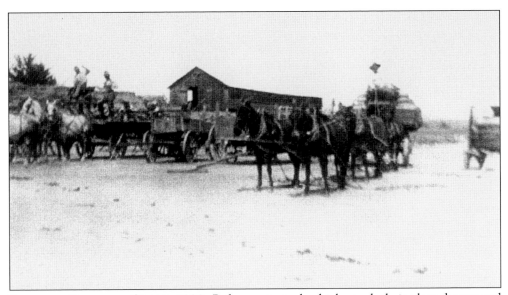

BRINGING HOME THE GRAIN, 1928. Before motorized vehicles took their place, horses and mules pulled wagons carrying people and products. In that era, a blacksmith held an important position on a ranch. After motorized vehicles became popular, automobile mechanics gradually took over. Few people still know how to hitch animals to wagons and very few know how to make horseshoes or how to nail them to the animal's hooves. (Courtesy of Edward G. Polley.)

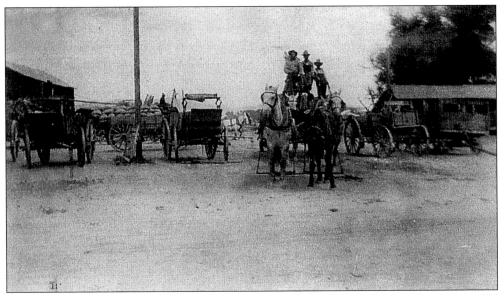

COMING IN FOR DINNER. After a long day's work, ranch hands looked forward to a bountiful evening meal in the Pauba Ranch cookhouse. Good meals were a perk when working for the Vails. (Courtesy of Edward G. Polley.)

CORN BINDER ON THE PAUBA/VAIL RANCH, 1925. A lone workman goes down a cornrow behind a horse, using a scythe to cut each corn stalk and bind the stalks together with baling wire. The horse drags the bound stalks to a wagon where they are taken for processing into the silage. (Courtesy of Edward G. Polley.)

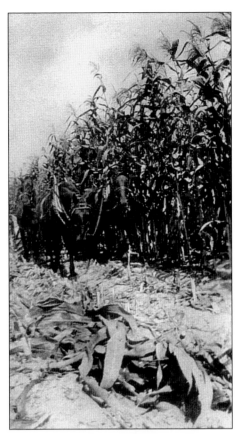

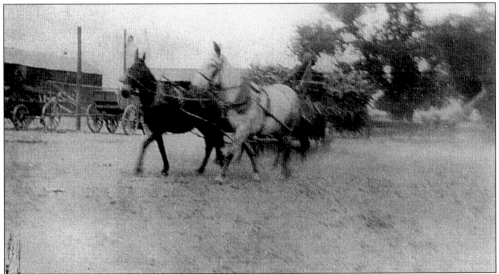

CORN FOR SILO. Horse-drawn wagons carry corn stalks to process at the ranch. Every bit of the stalk and ear of corn was ground for silage and stored in tall, cylindrical storage units called silos to protect the fodder from disintegration by heat and mold. After cattle grazed on open pastureland, silage was mixed with molasses and other grains to make feed to fatten the animals for market. (Courtesy of Edward G. Polley.)

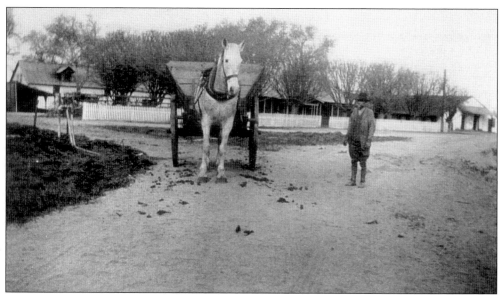

WHITE HORSE AND MANURE CART AT VAIL RANCH, 1920s. The many horses and mules on the Vail Ranch generated a lot of manure. This cart sitting in front of the cookhouse, with the Wolf Store in the background, looks like a manure cart, probably used to remove manure from the barns of the work animals. (Courtesy of Sandy Wilkinson.)

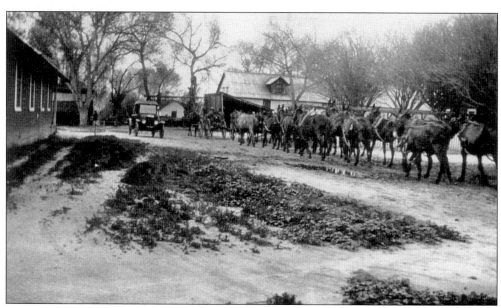

TWENTY-MULE TEAM AT VAIL RANCH. During the transition to mechanized farming and transportation, this photograph features a 1926 Model T Ford automobile, a horse-drawn wagon, and a 20-mule team. This photograph was taken from the Old Butterfield Stage Trail at the east end of the bunkhouse in the work yard near the cookhouse. (Courtesy of Sandy Wilkinson.)

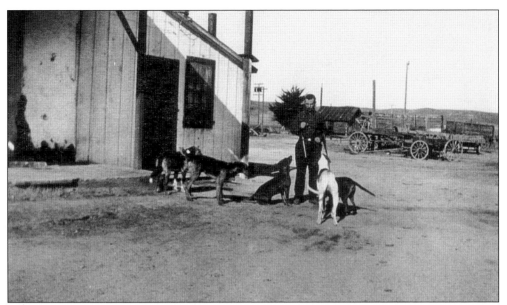

MAN WITH DOGS BY WOLF STORE. It looks like this unidentified man is preparing his dogs and shotguns for hunting birds. Game was plentiful throughout the valley with many varieties of fowl. This picture of the Wolf Store shows the north awning enclosed. During the Vail Ranch era, the building was used to store feed and tack. (Courtesy of Sandy Wilkinson.)

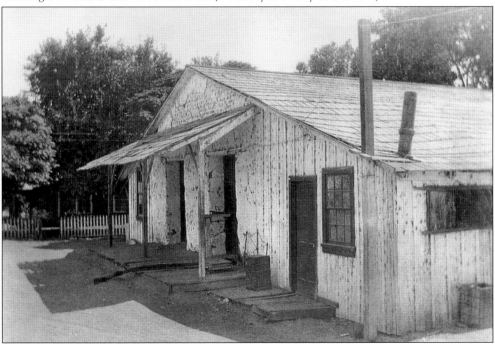

WOLF STORE ADOBE, 1940s. The adobe that had once been the Temecula Post Office, stage stop, general store, and hostelry served in the humble capacity of a storage shed during the Vail Ranch years. Its thick walls provided insulation for livestock feed or seed stored inside. Louis Wolf kept a scale on the porch to weigh bulk purchases at his store and one was used in the Vail Ranch era to weigh grain. (Courtesy of Sandy Wilkinson.)

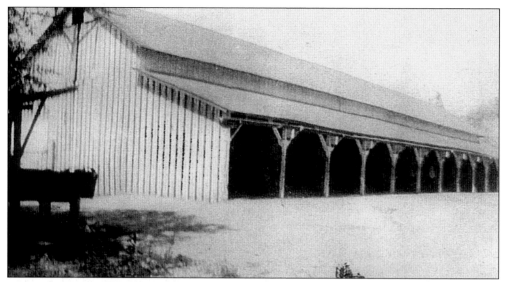

STABLES AT VAIL RANCH, 1925. Before complete implementation of mechanized farming equipment, horses and mules provided the power to transport men and non-motorized machines to work locations in fields on the ranch. There were several stables and barns at the ranch. This 4,800-square-foot stable burned to the ground in 1929. (Courtesy of Edward G. Polley.)

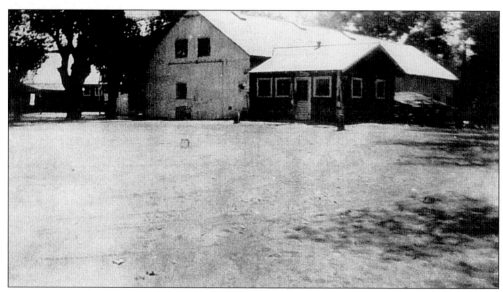

RED BARN AND OFFICE. During the Vail Ranch era, the small extension on the barn housed the ranch office. Workers would line up at the beginning of a workday to get their work assignments and to check out the equipment needed. They would also get their paychecks from this office. For many years, Frank Santa Maria worked as the blacksmith in the portion of the barn next to the office and the rest of the barn was a machine shop. In 1998, the barn was dismantled and rebuilt in its present location east of the bunkhouse. (Courtesy of Edward G. Polley.)

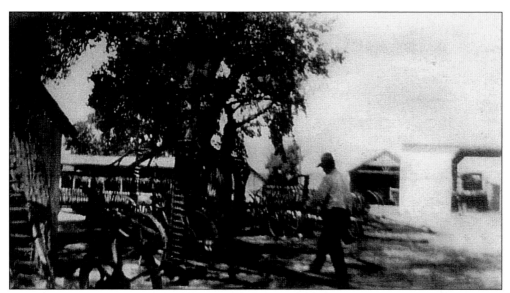

J. O. Freeman, Vail Ranch Foreman, 1925. James Oliver Freeman was born in 1882, the same year the railroad came to Temecula. He was foreman of the Pauba/Vail Ranch during the 1920s and served the community of Temecula in many capacities. Although the land for the Temecula Public Cemetery was deeded to the town from Mercedes Pujol in 1884, J. O. was one of the three men who organized the management of the cemetery. (Courtesy of Edward G. Polley.)

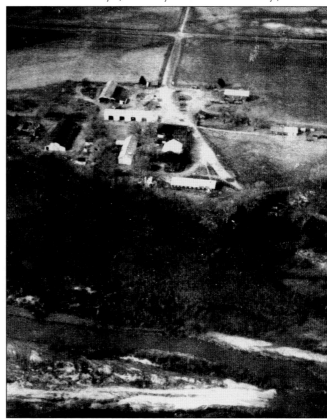

Aerial View of the Pauba Headquarters, 1918. Because the Vail Ranch spanned most of the countryside, specific areas were identified. The Vail Ranch Headquarters was located on a former Mexican land grant called Rancho Pauba, so it was called the Pauba Ranch Headquarters. This headquarters was the management seat of all of the Temecula area ranchos owned by the Vails. This photograph was taken by Dr. Ford A. Carpenter. (Courtesy of Sandy Wilkinson.)

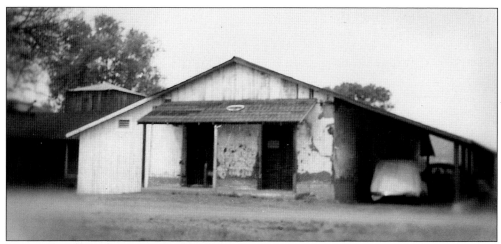

THE DOBE. The Dobe (rhymes with robe) is what cowboys and ranch hands called this building during the 1940s. The building has changed very little since this 1940s photograph was taken, with the exception of the addition of a brass plaque between the two front doors. The plaque, unveiled to a large audience on October 1, 1950, commemorates the signing of a peace treaty in 1852 at a nearby location. The treaty, signed by representatives of the federal government and 29 American Native tribes, was never ratified by Congress. (Courtesy of Robert Roripaugh.)

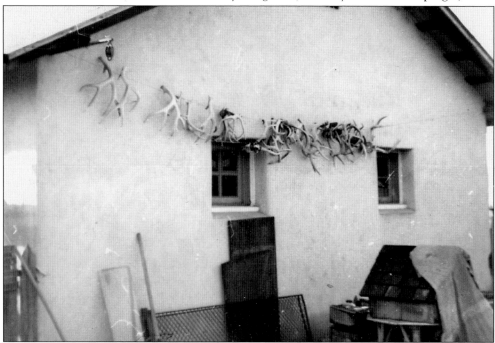

STRING OF ANTLERS ON FOREMAN'S HOUSE AT VAIL RANCH. This 1950 photograph shows 20 to 30 sets of deer antlers hanging from a line on the back of the adobe portion of the foreman's house. The 1998 demolition of this portion of the historical building at the Vail Ranch headquarters site prompted VaRRA to initiate a lawsuit against the County of Riverside and the owner of the property. The County of Riverside claimed the building was constructed in 1956, contrary to this photographic evidence and personal testimony attesting its construction in 1926, with adobe left from Casa Loma. (Courtesy of Robert Roripaugh.)

"DOC" AND HORSE. Harvey "Doc" Freeman was the son of Vail Ranch foreman James O. Freeman. He grew up to be the "best cowboy of the family." (Courtesy of Edward G. Polley.)

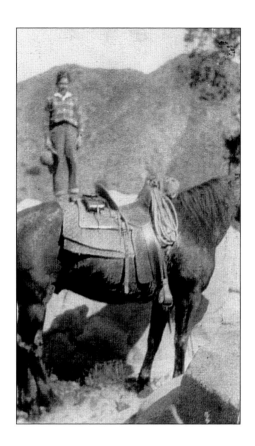

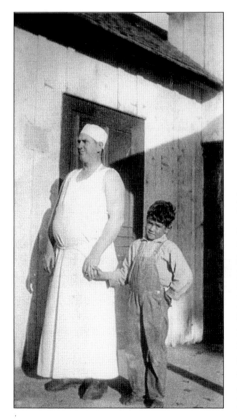

MALE COOK AND JULE FREEMAN OUTSIDE THE COOKHOUSE. Cooks were important to the morale of the ranch. In the absence of modern day restaurants, it was a treat to be invited to eat at the ranch. Besides the good meals, coffee and pie were always abundantly available. The cook in this photograph is unidentified. The child is Jule (pronounced "Hoole") Freeman, the youngest son of the foreman. Although there were several good cooks at the ranch through the years, some reportedly proved unreliable after they started drinking vanilla, which had a high alcohol content. Mahlon Vail hired replacements from an employment agency in Riverside. (Courtesy of Edward G. Polley.)

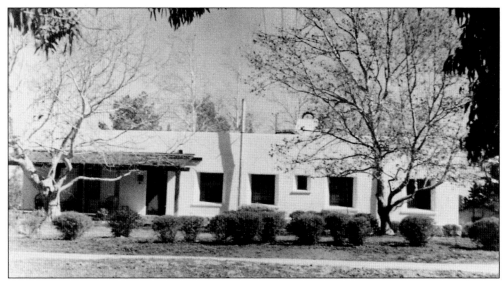

CASA LOMA, FRONT VIEW. In 1926, Mahlon Vail built his single-story adobe home on the hill overlooking the Vail Ranch. Interior stairs gave access to the roof so his wife could sunbathe. Mrs. Vail did not like living in Temecula. She preferred Los Angeles. Louie Roripaugh, foreman of the Vail Ranch, and his wife, Hedy, lived in Casa Loma for many years. Sometime after 1967, a second floor was added to provide two more bedrooms. A nearly straight line can be drawn between the Vail Ranch headquarters site, Casa Loma, the Wolf Monument, and the second Magee Store. (Courtesy of VaRRA.)

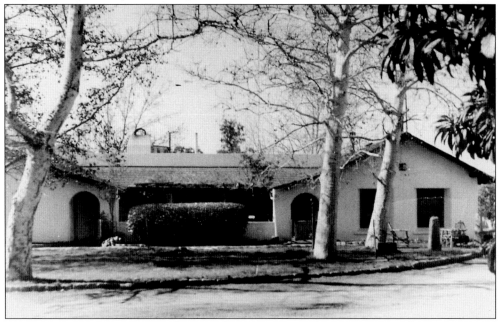

CASA LOMA, VIEW FROM BACK. The adobe house, constructed on a granite foundation, is a typical hacienda with an open courtyard between a bedroom wing on the left and a kitchen wing on the right. The third side, shown in the previous photograph, houses the living room, dining room, and master bedroom. Six fireplaces warm the house that features redwood floors and hand-hewn round timbers. A beautiful old wisteria vine graces the courtyard. (Courtesy of VaRRA.)

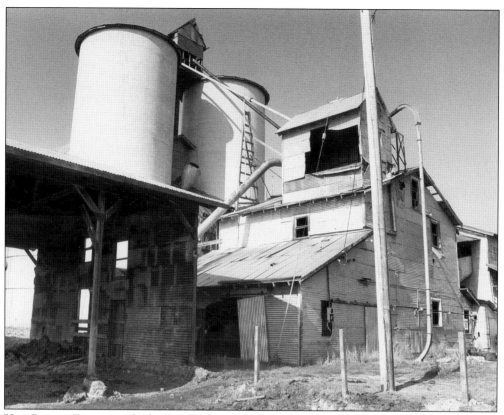

VAIL RANCH FEEDLOT. The feedlot and dairy were located near where the Home Depot Store is now on Highway 79 South. A pet goat at Upper Camp near the feedlot learned that she could drink from one of the drains on the side of the silo. The liquid draining from the fermenting silage made her tipsy and she had a hard time walking straight after imbibing the brew. (Courtesy of VaRRA.)

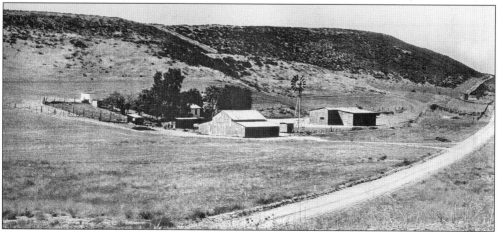

YODER CAMP. This picture shows only a small part of the 7,000 acres M. J. Yoder leased from the Vail Ranch. He raised barley and paid his lease with one-fourth of his crop. The dirt road was called Long Valley Road. It was a country road, with a lot of gates to open and close along the way. Yoder Camp is now the Maurice Car'rie Winery and the paved road is Rancho California Road. (Courtesy of Sandy Wilkinson.)

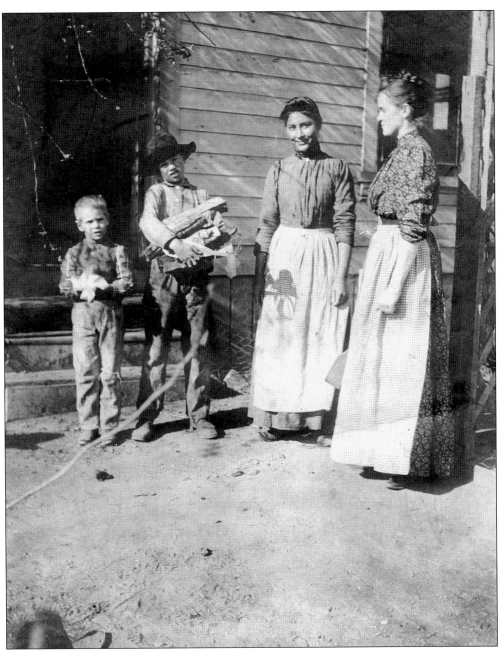

FAMILY AT PAUBA, LATE 1890s. Everyone at the Culver and Cobb Ranch contributed to the work. Olive Mabel Culver White Cobb's husband, Franklin Cobb, operated a cattle enterprise with her brother Watson Culver, leasing part of the Pauba Ranch. Franklin adopted his 15-year-old stepson, David, one month before Olive died at age 36 from tuberculosis. Franklin died two years later at the age of 49. The boy on the far left is an unidentified "orphan who lived with the family temporarily" and the second from the right was a domestic helper, "perhaps a Pechanga Indian." David White, second from the left, gave extensive details about cattle drives from the ranch in a 1957 interview. (Courtesy of Culver family.)

Seven

RANCHING BEYOND
THE PAUBA

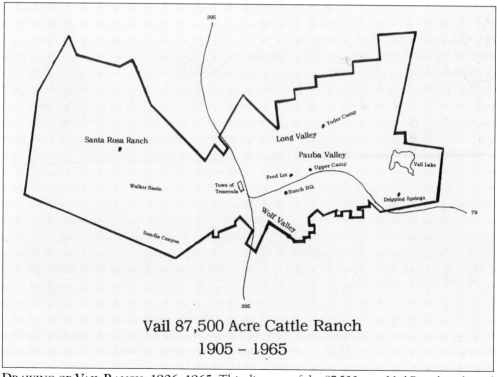

Vail 87,500 Acre Cattle Ranch
1905 – 1965

DRAWING OF VAIL RANCH, 1906–1965. This diagram of the 87,500-acre Vail Ranch is shaped like an eagle in flight. The ranch spanned from Camp Pendleton on the west to past Vail Lake in the east. It went from Highway 79 South to Clinton Keith Road. (Courtesy of VaRRA.)

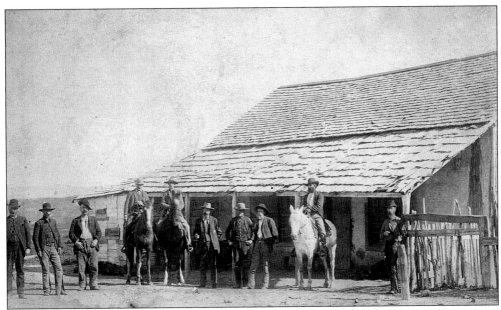

COWBOYS AND VISITORS TO SANTA ROSA RANCHO, 1890S. Parker Dear lost the Santa Rosa Rancho to the San Francisco Union Savings Bank. The gentlemen on horseback stand next to one of the structures on the rancho. It was one of the five mainland ranches later owned by the Vail Company. It is presently an ecological preserve managed by the Nature Conservancy. (Courtesy of Peggy Goffman.)

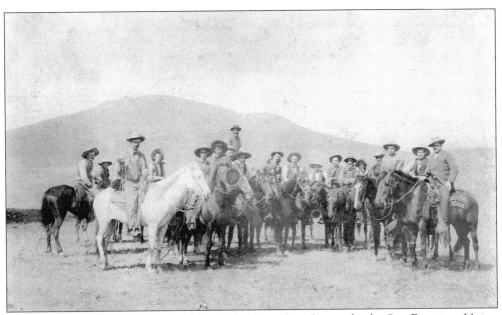

COWBOYS READY FOR ROUNDUP. After Parker Dear lost the ranch, the San Francisco Union Savings Bank rounded up all his cattle and branded them with a new mark. These unidentified cowboys are dressed with wide brimmed hats to shade their eyes from the sun and to prevent sunburn. The ropes coiled on their saddles are ready for the roundup, and the cowboy on the white horse is ready to throw his lasso. (Courtesy of Peggy Goffman.)

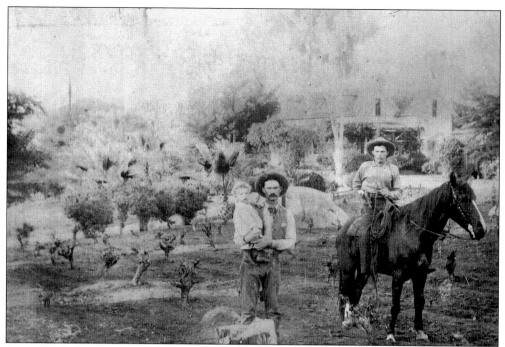

SANTA ROSA VINEYARD. James "Jim" Knight, foreman of the Santa Rosa Ranch, poses with one of his children and his brother in the vineyard in front of the ranch house. He was born in Texas, became the foreman for the Vail Company when they leased grazing land in Warner Springs, and eventually worked as foreman at the Santa Rosa Ranch. He is buried in the Temecula Cemetery. (Courtesy of Peggy Goffman.)

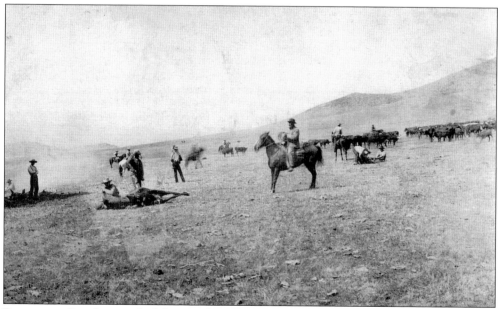

BRANDING. Ranchers marked their cattle with a personal brand by burning the hide with a piece of iron shaped with their mark. The Vails branded their cattle with a heart on the left back flank. (Courtesy of Peggy Goffman.)

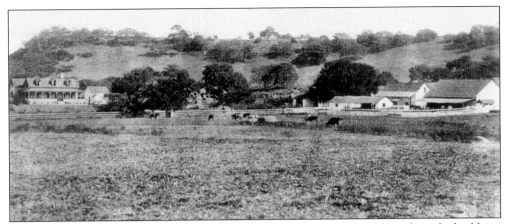

PANORAMA OF SANTA ROSA RANCH HOUSE. This sweeping panorama shows how the buildings at the Santa Rosa Ranch looked in the 1890s. The grand home on the left was built by Parker Dear. An adobe tack shed, possibly one of the earliest buildings in Riverside County, is to the left of the barns, and Augustin Machado's adobe is the second building from the right. The Santa Rosa Ranch was valuable pastureland, first for Juan Moreno's sheep and later for the Vail cattle. (Courtesy of Santa Rosa Plateau Ecological Reserve.)

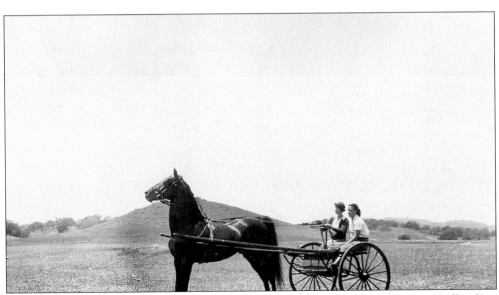

MARGARET VAIL BELL WITH HORSE AND CART. Margaret and her niece, Barbara Bell, take a ride across the rolling pastureland of the Santa Rosa Ranch during a family visit to the ranch in the 1930s. (Courtesy of VaRRA.)

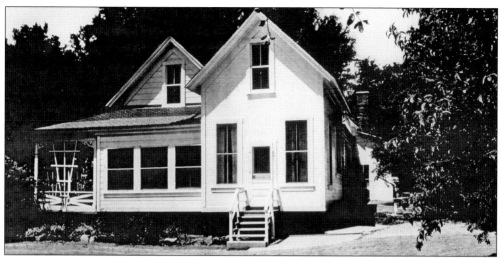

NORTH SIDE OF SANTA ROSA RANCH HOUSE, 1950S. The Vails did not use this ranch house, formerly the Parker Dear house, except when they visited from Los Angeles. They would ride the train to Temecula and stay the night at the Temecula Hotel before traveling approximately 20 miles to the Santa Rosa Ranch. For many years, Joe Gomez, the foreman of the ranch, and his wife, Mary, lived in a cottage behind the big house. Mary cooked for ranch hands and visitors to the ranch. (Courtesy of Santa Rosa Plateau Ecological Reserve.)

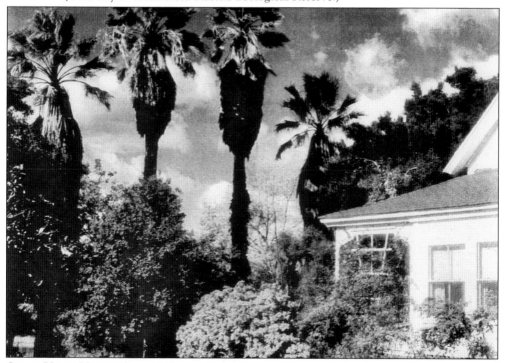

CLOSE UP OF NORTH SIDE OF SANTA ROSA RANCH HOUSE. Parker Dear, an Englishman, and his wife, the former Elena Couts, designed their home with great care and surrounded it with beautiful trees and plants. Each year on May 1, the Dears invited neighbors and friends from far and wide to join them for a picnic and barbecue at their ranch. The house burned down in the 1970s. (Courtesy of Sandy Wilkinson.)

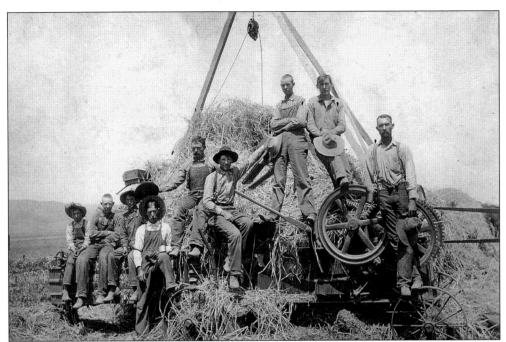

HAYING CREW ON PAUBA RANCH, 1890S. This group of boys and men are posing on a hay baler. It took four men to run the machine. James Knight, at the far right, was foreman of the Warner Ranch and Santa Rosa Ranch. He lost his right arm when a wagon he was riding in hit a bump and a shotgun went off. (Courtesy of Peggy Goffman.)

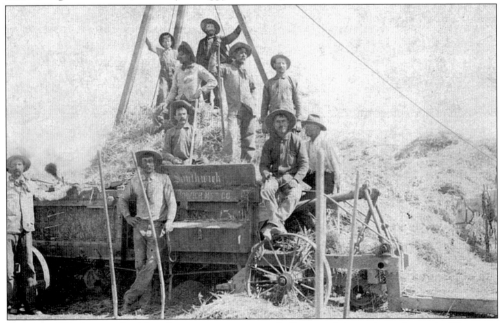

HAYING. Workers pitched hay from a wagon onto a baling machine using a jerry rig. Two men stuffed hay into the chute using chompers. Another man poked wires into spacers to form each bale. Steam engines with 50-foot-long belts operated early balers. Gas engines later replaced the steam engines. (Courtesy of Peggy Goffman.)

FRANK SANTA MARIA ON A MULE. Frank Santa Maria, born in 1921, said he would rather ride a mule than a horse any day because mules were smarter. Frank was a blacksmith for the Vail Ranch and worked in the barn at the Pauba/Vail Ranch headquarters site. He rented space in the barn to blacksmith and do mechanical work after the ranch was sold. He was the last worker to leave the ranch. (Courtesy of Knott family.)

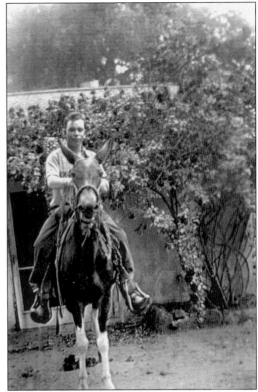

EARLY PAUBA BRANDING—CASTRATING AND DEHORNING. These Pauba Ranch cowboys hold down a young bull to remove its horns and begin castration. Removing the horns prevents injury to other cattle and castration renders the animal less aggressive and easier to handle. (Courtesy of Jim Ramsay.)

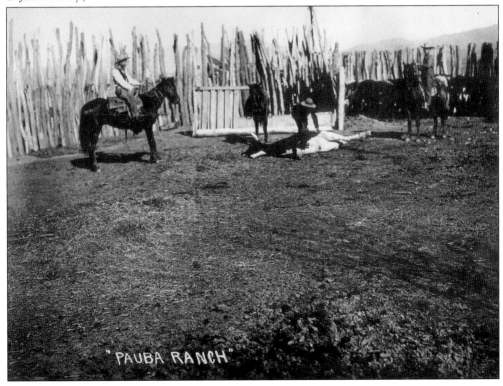

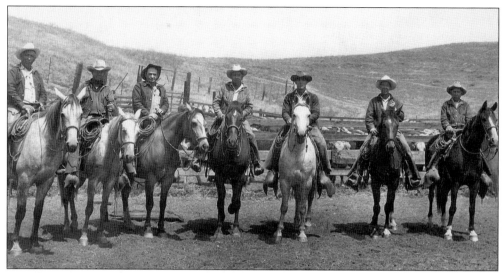

VAIL RANCH COWBOYS, 1947. This photograph was taken at the feedlot near the north side of the present-day Highway 79 South. The cowboys are Reyes Laborin, Rafael Villa, Ben Kane, Joe Gomez, Janaro Bernel, Carlos Reyes, and Chappo Labato. In a 1984 interview, Joe Gomez said, "The cowboys would herd the cattle on horseback. Once, seven of us drove maybe a thousand head to the lots, then, we all lined up on our horses to have our picture taken. Sam Hicks took the picture." This photograph, referred to as "The Magnificent Seven," is reproduced on a billboard attached to the Kohl's Department store in Temecula. (Courtesy of Sandy Wilkinson.)

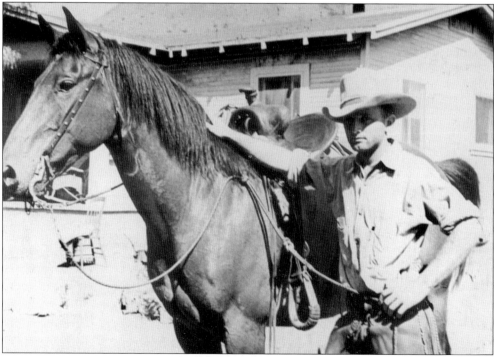

YOUNG LOUIE RORIPAUGH. Louis "Louie" Roripaugh (1907–1994) grew up in a ranching family. His wide brimmed hat shaded his eyes and protected his head. The cowboys wore felt hats in the winter for warmth and used straw hats in the summer. (Courtesy of VaRRA.)

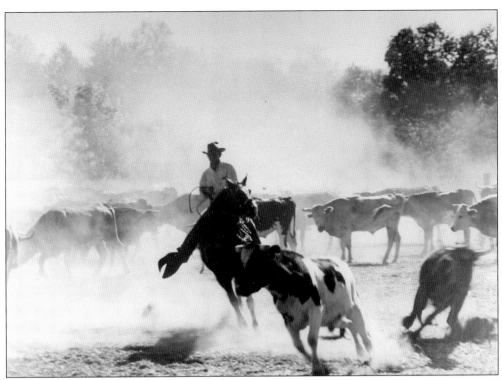

LOUIE RORIPAUGH CUTTING THE CATTLE, 1950S. Louie Roripaugh is hard at work cutting cattle, separating them from the herd. Leather chaps were worn over trousers to protect skin and clothing from tearing on chaparral. The ranches raised about 7,000 cattle each year. (Courtesy of VaRRA.)

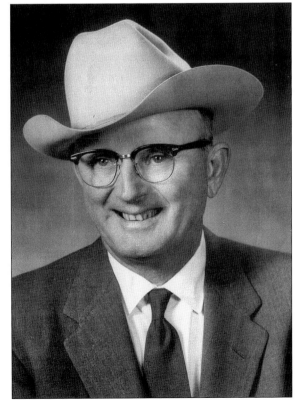

LOUIE RORIPAUGH, FOREMAN AND MANAGER OF VAIL RANCH. Louie supervised up to 50 ranch employees. He traveled the western United States, from Mexico to Montana, to buy yearling calves to fatten on the ranch. He married Hedy Burger, a secretary to author Erle Stanley Gardner. They made their home at Casa Loma for many years. When the Vail Ranch sold, he worked for Macco Realty and Kaiser Aluminum, the new owners. The Vails turned over their heart brand to Louie. (Courtesy of Sandy Wilkinson.)

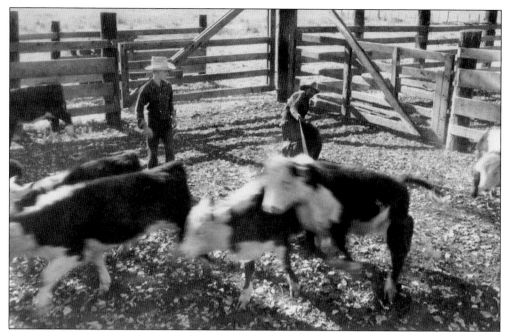

JIM RAMSAY IN PEN. 4-H member Jim Ramsay watches cowboy Joe Gomez rope a calf. Joe and his wife, Mary, worked for the Vail Company for many years. Joe was foreman of the Santa Rosa Ranch, and Mary cooked for the ranch hands. She also cooked at author Erle Stanley Gardner's Rancho del Paisano. After the Vail Ranch sold, Joe continued working as a cowboy for Louie Roripaugh. Joe retired after spending 39 years in the saddle. (Courtesy of Jim Ramsay.)

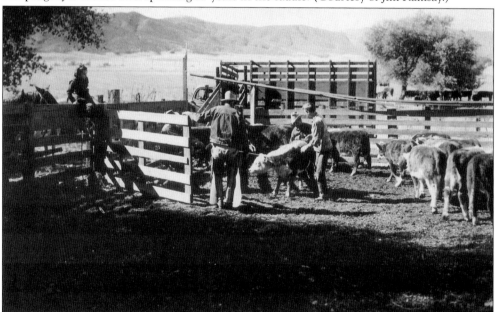

JIM AND 4-H CALVES. Each year the Vail Ranch provided calves for 4-H Club members. Jim is in the pen guiding a calf through the gate while Louise Roripaugh, Louie's daughter, encourages him from her seat on the fence. The cowboy near the gate was Julio, who also worked at the Santa Rosa Ranch. (Courtesy of Jim Ramsay.)

VAIL RANCH COWBOYS DIPPING CATTLE, 1950S. Cowboys lead the cattle down a chute to be dipped in a pesticide solution called rotenone, used to protect the animals from ticks and other insects. Often the cowboys would dip, inoculate, castrate, brand, and notch the ears of the cattle in one long process. (Courtesy of James Ramsay.)

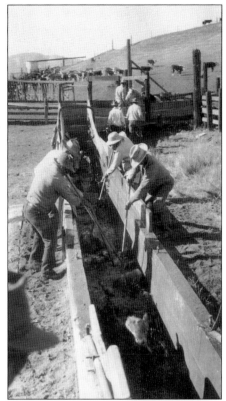

COWBOYS TALKING. Louie Roripaugh, Ben Kane, and Dick Ramsay discuss the day's activities at the corral across the road from the Pauba feedlot. In one area of the ranch was a "bone yard," where discarded parts were saved for later use, including brass acetylene headlights from old vehicles, old buggy lights, and a mix of other things. In the nearby harness room were bins of copper rivets, tools, leather, snaps, rings, buckles, and other hardware. In 1939, gasoline was about 20¢ a gallon. (Courtesy of Jim Ramsay.)

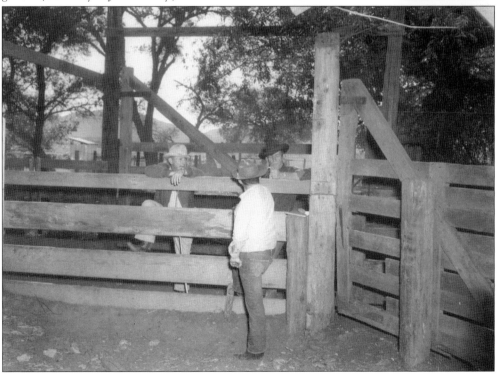

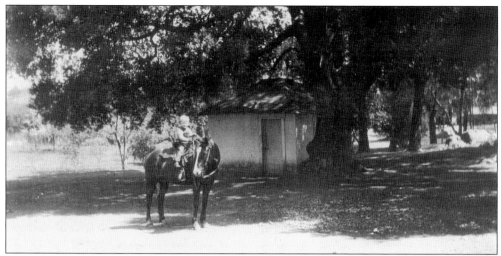

SANDY WILKINSON AT SANTA ROSA RANCH, 1923. James Vail "Sandy" Wilkinson, grandson of Walter Vail, rides a horse while visiting the Santa Rosa Ranch. In the background is the Juan Moreno adobe and some large old oaks that still stand. The Nature Conservancy presently owns 7,000 acres of the former ranch as part of the Santa Rosa Plateau Ecological Reserve. The group protects the rare and endangered plants, oaks, and vernal pools located on the property. (Courtesy of Santa Rosa Plateau Ecological Reserve.)

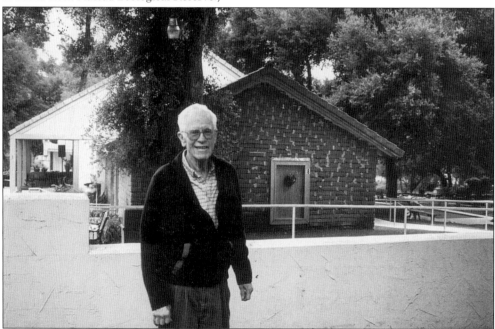

SANDY WILKINSON AT MAHLON VAIL'S HUNTING RETREAT, 2001. Sandy Wilkinson stands in front his uncle's adobe hunting retreat near the Vail Dam. It is at the extreme eastern portion of the 87,500-acre Vail Ranch, along the Butterfield Stage Route near the watering hole at Dripping Springs. Mahlon Vail enjoyed hunting and entertaining friends from Los Angeles at his rustic hideaway. When the ranch sold in the 1960s, this area was developed into a family campground and entertainment center called Butterfield Country. It is now the Vail Lake Resort. (Courtesy of VaRRA.)

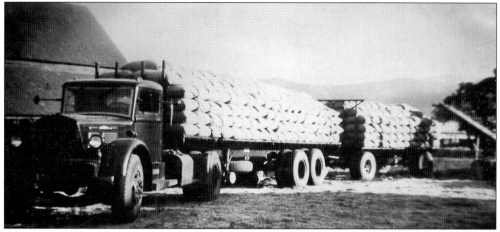

GRAIN TRUCK. Dick Evans owned a trucking business in Temecula and hauled grain for local farmers. Here are 100-pound sacks of barley from Leo Roripaugh's ranch. They were thrown onto the truck by hand. Two men held each sack and gave it a heave ho. This barley was headed to a mill in Colton. After World War II, barley was stored in silos and shipped to market in bulk. (Courtesy of June Roripaugh Tull.)

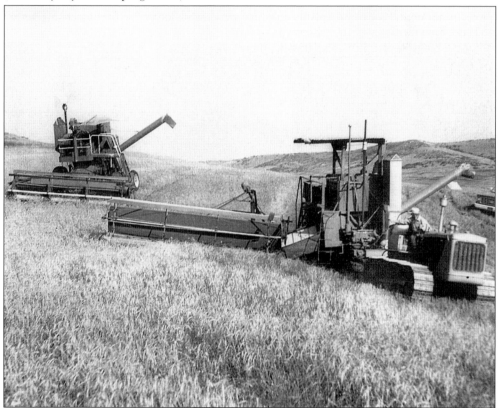

HARVESTING. These two harvesters were owned by Leo Roripaugh. The one in the foreground is pulled by a D-6 Caterpillar, a two-man operation. The second harvester is a self-propelled pusher that could be operated by one man. About 100 acres could be harvested in a day, working from dawn to dusk. (Courtesy of Jack Roripaugh.)

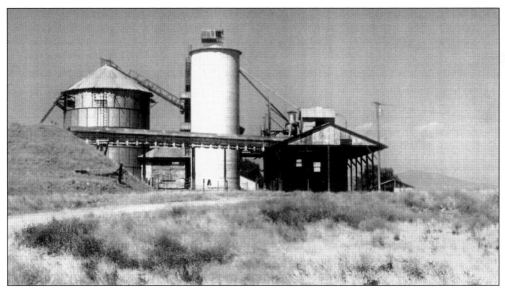

FEEDLOT. Careful records were kept of cattle purchases, sales, and losses. A logbook recorded when animals were moved from one pasture to another and when changes were made to their diets. Louie Roripaugh's 1939 logbook shows how many sacks of grain were taken to each pasture and how many head of cattle were in each. It also records when the cattle from each pasture was dipped in pesticide. (Courtesy of VaRRA.)

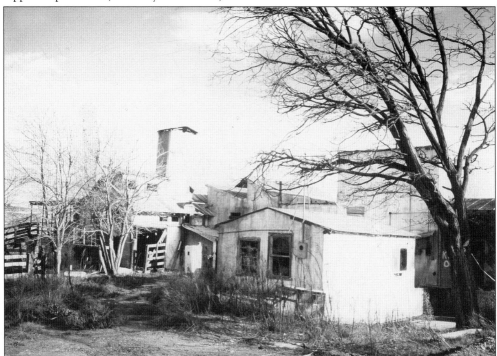

SLAUGHTERHOUSE. Bill Friedemann owned the slaughterhouse that stood on the west bank of Murrieta Creek, just south of town. He also owned the meat market. In 1928, the original slaughterhouse burned down. The rebuilt structure continued to serve the community through the 1950s. (Courtesy of VaRRA.)

Eight

FROM RANCHING TO TODAY

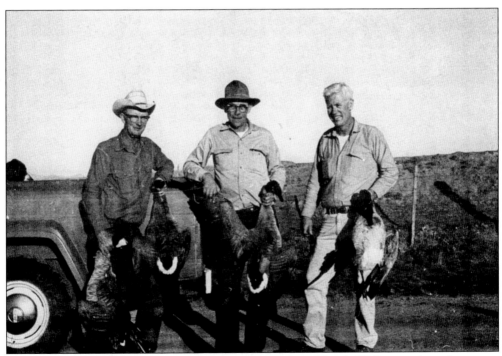

AFTER THE HUNT, 1950S. Leo Roripaugh, Alex Borel, and Sandy Wilkinson show their geese from a hunt in the Temecula Valley. Because of the abundant water in the valley, there was also a bountiful supply of game. Mahlon Vail entertained many friends at the ranch by taking them hunting. These friends included Donald Douglas, General Omar Bradley, Ty Cobb, and Hal Roach. (Courtesy of Sandy Wilkinson.)

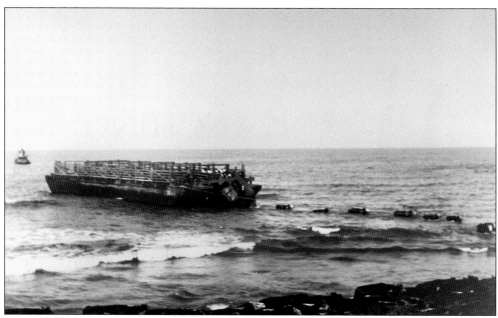

CATTLE SWIMMING TO SHORE FROM VAQUERO AT SANTA ROSA ISLAND, 1940. The Vail Company transported as many as 500 calves or 250 adult animals at a time in *Vaquero*, their first cattle barge, between Ventura or Santa Barbara and their ranch on Santa Rosa Island in the Channel Islands. They made their runs at night so they wouldn't lose a day of work. Built in 1913, the barge ran until it was taken for combat duty in the South Pacific in 1943. (Courtesy of VaRRA.)

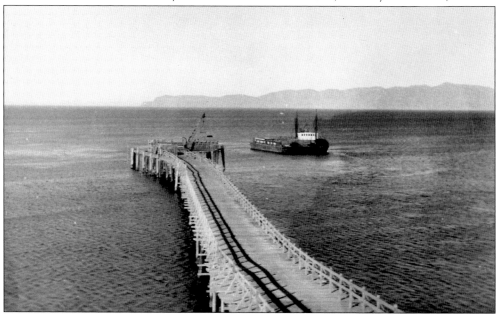

SANTA ROSA ISLAND PIER. With the lack of natural harbors on Santa Rosa Island, the Vail Company built a pier to load and unload cargo. The Vails purchased the uninhabited Channel Island, off the coast from Santa Barbara or Ventura, which was originally inhabited by Chumash Indians in 1901. The island offered verdant grazing on wild oats, clover, and other grasses. (Courtesy of Robert Roripaugh.)

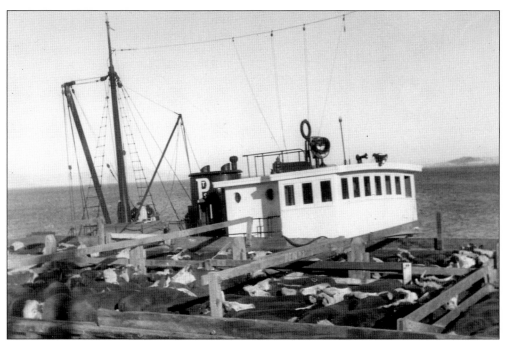

VAQUERO II. Cattle in pens on the *Vaquero II* approach Santa Rosa Island. Yearlings were first transported to the island in 1891. It is sometimes confusing to learn the Vail Company owned both the Santa Rosa Island off the coast of the Channel Islands and also owned the Santa Rosa Ranch in Riverside County. (Courtesy of Robert Roripaugh.)

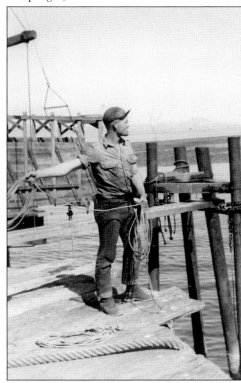

ROBERT RORIPAUGH ROPING. Robert Roripaugh heaves a line to *Vaquero II* as it approaches the pier at Santa Rosa Island. Robert helped build the main road on the island that made motor vehicle travel possible there. The Vails built hay barns, a bunkhouse, and a ranch house on the windswept island. (Courtesy of Robert Roripaugh.)

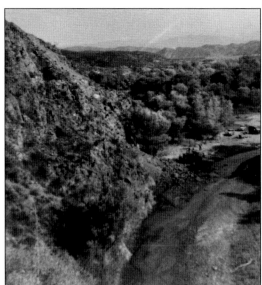

CANYON BEFORE THE DAM. The canyon had a tragic history before the Vails built the dam that flooded the canyon to form Vail Lake. Old maps identify it as "Nigger Canyon." In January 1847, some ranchers and a neighboring Indian tribe with a vendetta enticed the Temecula Indians to enter the canyon, then ambushed them, massacring somewhere between 40 and 120 Temecula Indians. The mass grave of the massacre victims is hidden behind a concrete wall on the south side of Highway 79 South. (Courtesy of Robert Roripaugh.)

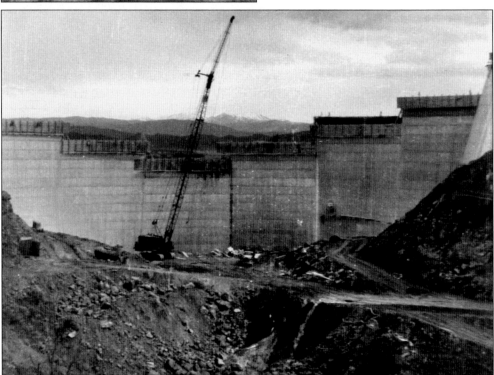

VAIL DAM UNDER CONSTRUCTION. Even before 1900, the Pauba Land and Water Company considered building a dam to supply water to ranchers in the Temecula Valley, but it was nearly 50 years before it was constructed. In 1924, the Rancho Santa Margarita filed a lawsuit to limit the amount of water the Vail Ranch used from the Temecula Creek. After an unfavorable judgment, the Vails appealed to the California State Supreme Court. In the eventual 1938 settlement, Rancho Santa Margarita received rights to two-thirds of the water while the Vail Ranch received the other third. It was the biggest water case in the United States up to that time and cost over $1 million in legal fees. (Courtesy of Robert Roripaugh.)

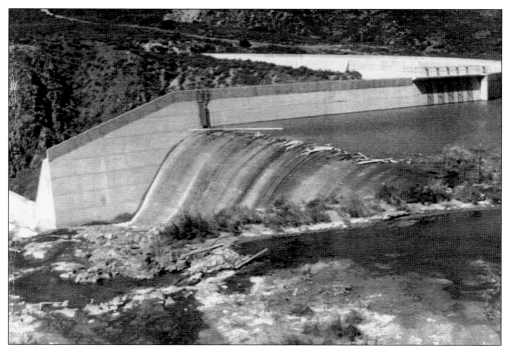

FINISHED DAM. The dam was completed in 1948 at a cost of more than $1 million. The dam is 750 feet long and 132 feet tall. A 10-mile-long pipeline delivers water for irrigation, ending at the entrance to Wolf Valley. It formed Vail Lake, a recreation area for boating and fishing. (Courtesy of Knott Family.)

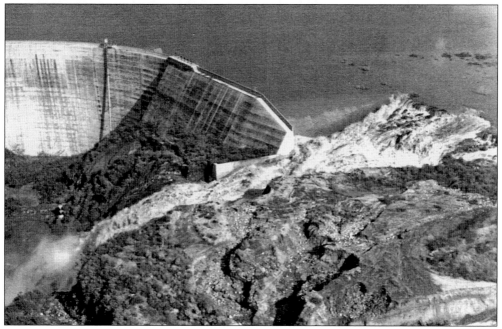

ANOTHER VIEW OF DAM. The dam is unique because its construction was not financed by government funds. Not only was it built by private money, it was also privately owned. Today the Vail Lake Resort offers camping facilities near the lake. (Courtesy of Knott Family.)

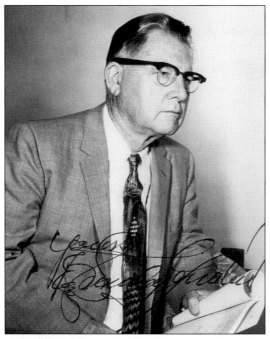

ERLE STANLEY GARDNER. Attorney/author Erle Stanley Gardner was one of Temecula's most famous residents. In the late 1930s, Gardner, author of the Perry Mason mysteries, bought Rancho del Paisano. As an attorney, he started "The Court of Last Resort" to defend people who he thought were falsely accused of crimes. Gardner wrote his last Perry Mason story in 1969 and died in 1970. (Courtesy of the Seay family.)

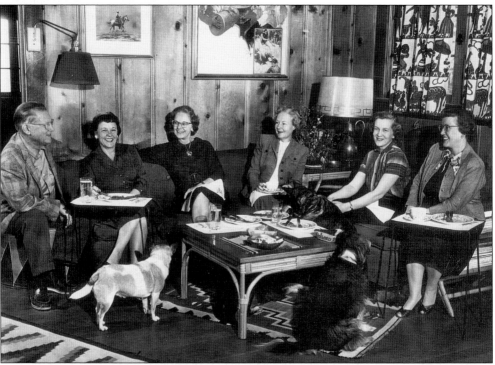

ERLE STANLEY GARDNER AND SECRETARIES. The prolific author dictated all of his work and kept five to seven secretaries busy transcribing his work. He wrote 131 novels, selling over 325 million copies. His stories were presented in 6 movies, 271 television episodes, and 3,221 radio programs. Pictured with him are Peggy Downs, Jean Bethell, Helene Seay, Ruth "Honey" Moore, and Millie Conarroe. (Courtesy of the Seay family.)

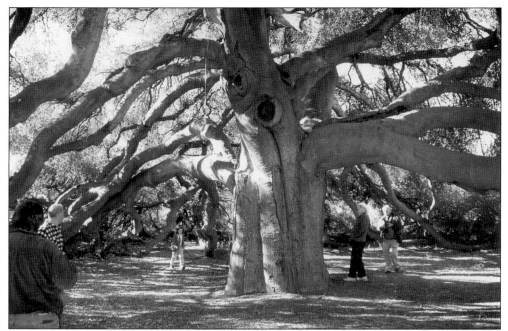

GREAT OAK. This tree on Rancho del Paisano is now part of the Pechanga Reservation and is considered a special place. It is so large that at first sight it looks like a grove of trees. It is 96 feet tall, with a branch span of 590 feet and a trunk that is nearly 20 feet in circumference. (Courtesy of VaRRA.)

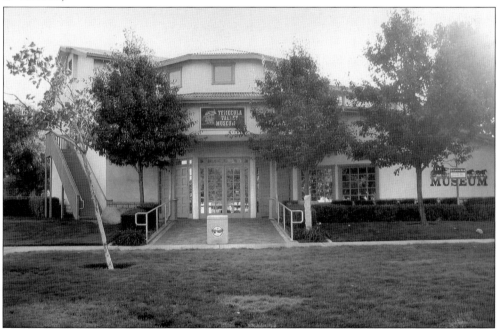

TEMECULA VALLEY MUSEUM. Tony Tobin collected artifacts for many years before opening the first museum in a storefront at Butterfield Square in 1985. The museum had two other locations before the City of Temecula built the current facility in Sam Hicks Monument. (Courtesy of Barnett collection.)

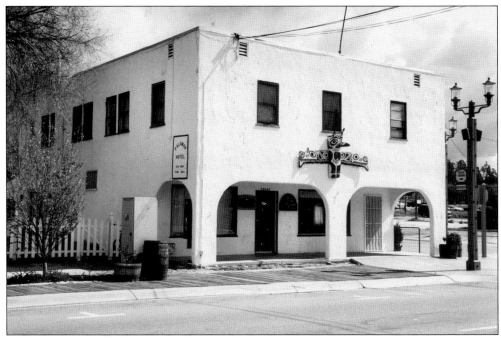

PALOMAR HOTEL. This hotel opened in 1928 as Hotel McCulloch. When Robert Majeski purchased the hotel in 1954, an Indian chief from Washington State gave his family the Thunderbird totem pole for good luck. Since 1928, the hotel has been in continuous operation, and rooms can still be rented. (Courtesy of VaRRA.)

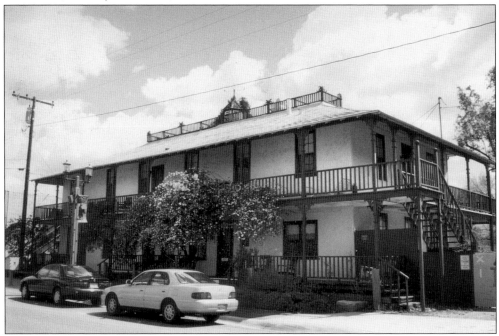

TEMECULA HOTEL. Constructed in 1891, this hotel replaced the first one that burned down. R. J. and Mary Jane Welty and their seven daughters operated it for over 30 years. More recently, it has been a private residence. (Courtesy of Horace and Leverne Parker Collection.)

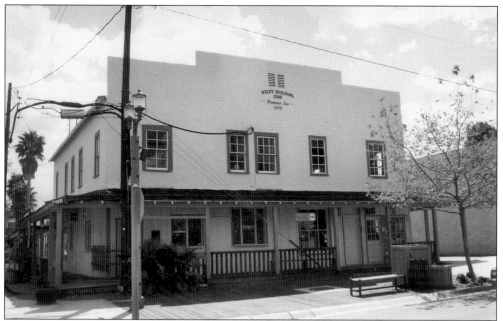

WELTY BUILDING. R. J. Welty constructed the building in the 1890s, using the lower floor for a store and renting out rooms upstairs. When Joe Winkles bought it during Prohibition, he renamed it the Ramona Inn and sold liquor illegally from the premises. It is now the home of the Temecula Olive Oil Company. (Courtesy of VaRRA.)

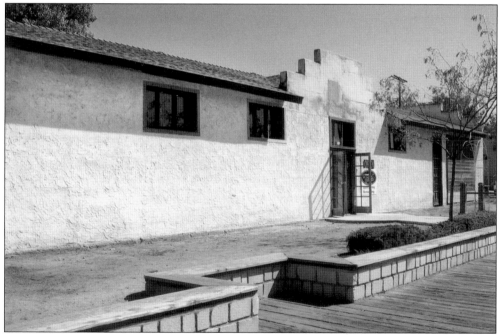

MACHADO BUILDING. When Louis Wolf moved his business from the Wolf Store to an area closer to the railroad, he partnered with "Mac" Machado. After Wolf died, Machado continued as a shopkeeper, often trading Indian baskets for the wares the patrons needed. This second building replaced a previous one that burned. It is presently an antique store. (Courtesy of Barnett collection.)

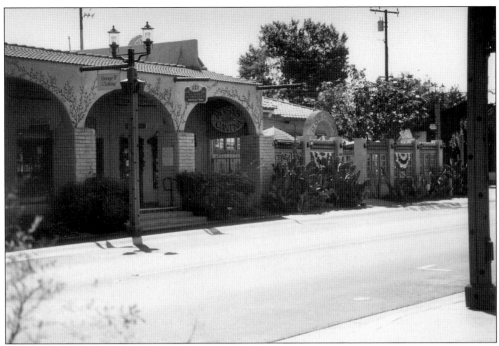

CHAMPION BUILDING. This building has been used for several different types of businesses, including a barbershop, a restaurant, and a bank. It served as the Temecula Post Office for a while until the Old Town Post Office opened two and a half blocks away in 1981. (Courtesy of VaRRA.)

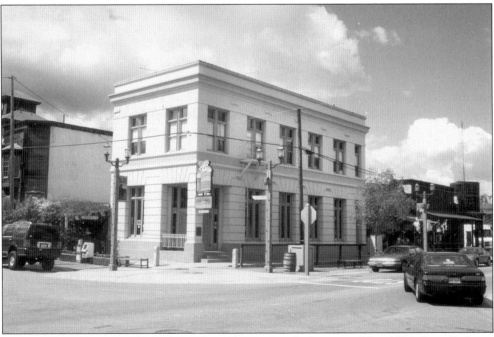

BANK. From 1914 to 1943, the bank conducted business at the location of the old McConville livery stable. The bank is now a Mexican restaurant and customers may dine inside the old vault where the bank cashier and teller were sent when the bank was robbed in 1930. (Courtesy of VaRRA.)

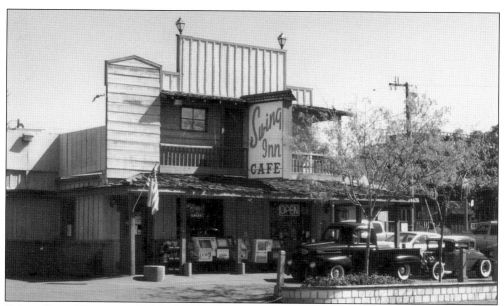

SWING INN. This restaurant on Front Street in Old Town Temecula, first known as Mothers Cafe, was started by Charles and Sarah Clogston. Sarah was a daughter of Eli Barnett. It was later called Alessandro's for the Temecula Indian character in Helen Hunt Jackson's novel *Ramona*. This restaurant has continued to serve good home cooked meals to the public since it opened in 1927. (Courtesy of VaRRA.)

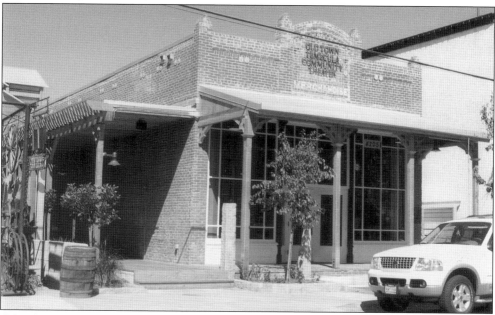

OLD TOWN TEMECULA COMMUNITY THEATER. The City of Temecula purchased the old Burnham or Mercantile Store in the 1990s and retrofitted it to meet state earthquake standards. In October 2005, it was reopened as the entry to a 362-seat community theater. Instead of selling general merchandise, the former Mercantile Store houses the ticket office and displays works of local artists in the entry gallery. A cozy meeting area between the theater and the ticket office is called "The Merc." (Courtesy of Barnett collection.)

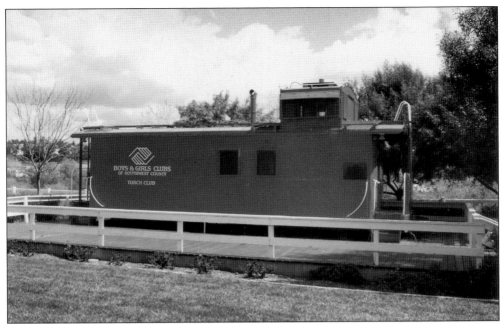

CABOOSE. George Buhler, a retired executive of the Atchison, Topeka & Santa Fe Railroad, arranged for the donation of the caboose to the Temecula Town Association. The proceeds from a 1983 fund-raiser supplied the money necessary to move the caboose to Temecula, where it was used as a public meeting room and later for the neighborhood police station. (Courtesy of VaRRA.)

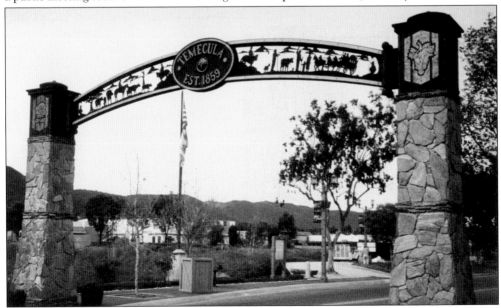

OLD TOWN ARCH. Arches grace the north and south ends of Old Town Temecula Front Street. Bob Morris, local historical architect and artist, designed the patterns of the arches to represent Temecula history. The tale of Temecula is told with symbols showing Native Americans, an oak tree, a stagecoach, a windmill, cattle, 1859 (to represent the year the first post office was established in Temecula), a rose (the symbol of the planned community of Rancho California), and grapes to represent the vineyards. (Courtesy of VaRRA.)

THEY PASSED THIS WAY MONUMENT.
The Temecula Valley Chamber
of Commerce sponsored the 1969
construction of this 150-ton monument.
Sam Hicks designed it from granite
donated by Frank and Odessa Quarry, and
Jack Roripaugh furnished the equipment.
Names of former luminaries who came
through or near Temecula are sand
blasted into the stone. The monument
is near the Temecula Valley Museum.
(Courtesy of VaRRA.)

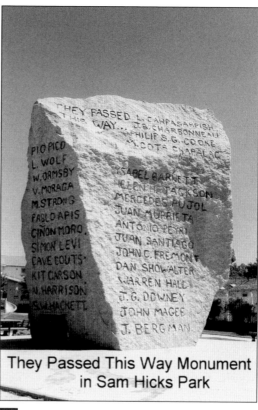

They Passed This Way Monument
in Sam Hicks Park

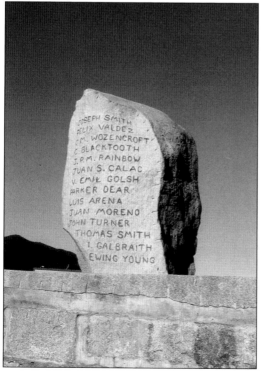

ANOTHER SIDE OF THE MONUMENT. In
Sam Hicks's words from a booklet titled
They Passed This Way, the monument
was erected "to honor the passing parade
of devoted frontier people who suffered
to bring this town its proud and wealthy
heritage and who, in some measure,
personally contributed to the subsequent
development of this historic valley." The
booklet listing the significance of each
person represented on the monument is
available for perusal inside the Temecula
Valley Museum on the first floor.
(Courtesy of VaRRA.)

125

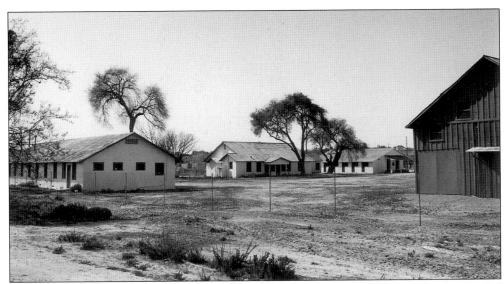

VAIL RANCH, 2005. Negotiations are presently underway to restore the buildings on this site and to make it into a community resource. There will be open parkland and commercial activity to complement historic reenactments and self-guided tours of the Temecula of yesteryear. (Courtesy of VaRRA.)

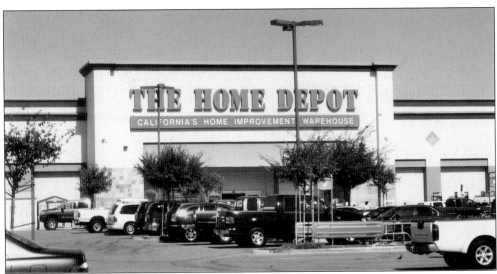

HOME DEPOT. This building sits close to where the old Vail Feedlot once stood. Robert Roripaugh recalls his first day working on the Vail Ranch in 1939. He and another worker climbed into the silo to spread the chopped corn as it was poured inside, using scoop shovels to spread even layers of corn. He was paid $1 and three bountiful meals a day. (Courtesy of VaRRA.)

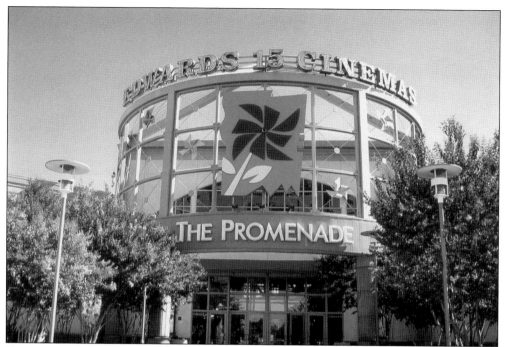

ENTRANCE TO PROMENADE MALL. The mall sits on land that used to be a potato field. Until the 1990s, Ynez and Winchester Roads were each just two lanes, with stop signs only on Ynez Road. Ynez Road is now six-lanes wide, and Winchester has eight lanes. (Courtesy of VaRRA.)

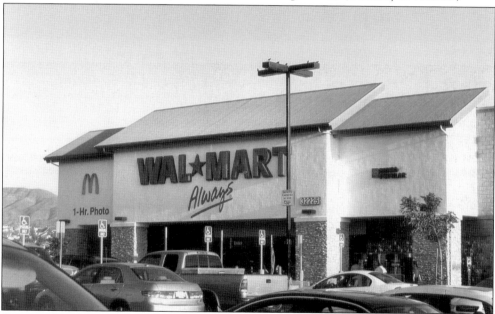

GENERAL MERCHANDISE STORE ON HIGHWAY 79 SOUTH. The land where this general merchandise store sits has been used as an alfalfa and potato field. It is adjacent to the historic Vail Ranch headquarters. A commercial cycle has come full circle with the opening of Wal-Mart in 2002 in close proximity to the Wolf Store, which was the area's commercial center in 1867. (Courtesy of VaRRA.)

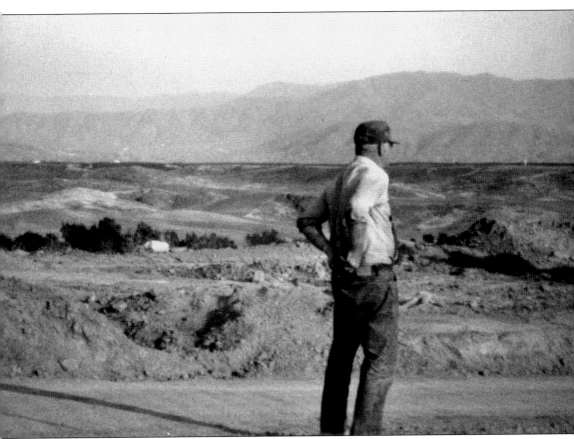

Leo Elmour Roripaugh Pondering the Future of Temecula Valley. A third-generation resident of the valley, bridging the past and future, Leo Roripaugh gazes across the open expanse of his property near Nicholas Road, before commercial and residential properties filled the countryside. Born in 1909 in his grandfather Eli Barnett's house, he had the run of the whole landscape as a child. He and Marian were married for 68 years and owned 3,000 acres of farmland. He passed away in 1999 after living his entire life in the Temecula Valley as a rancher and farmer. His legacy lives on. (Courtesy of June Roripaugh Tull.)